YO-DAF-523

A SEASON OF SAINTS

Sermons For Festivals And
Commemorations After Pentecost

BY JOHN P. ROSSING

C.S.S Publishing Co., Inc.
Lima, Ohio

A SEASON OF SAINTS

Library of Congress Cataloging-in-Publication Data

Rossing, John P., 1956-
    A season of saints : sermons for festivals and commemorations after Pentecost / by John P. Rossing.
        p.   cm.
    Includes bibliographical references.
    ISBN 1-55673-408-5
    1. Sermons, American.   2. Festival-day sermons.   I. Title.
BV4254.3.R67   1992
252'67—dc20   91-26962
                                                                        CIP

9221 / ISBN 1-55673-408-5   PRINTED IN U.S.A.

To the memory of my parents, Robert and Lynette Rossing, the first saints I knew.

Table Of Contents

Preface

I owe my gratitude to the members of All Saints Lutheran Church in Lilburn, Georgia, and to their pastor, Matthew Ernst. Their appreciation for the church catholic, their commitment to the "faith once delivered to the saints," and their acknowledgment of their debt to their spiritual forebears are all reflected in their love of historical commemorations. I thank them for the invitation to prepare and deliver meditations for those commemorations; I thank them also for their constant friendship and support.

Introduction

Between Pentecost and Advent the church observes a long green season. The Sundays after Pentecost — roughly June through November — are often called the Half-year of the Church, in contrast to the Half-year of the Lord, the first half of the church year during which all the major festivals commemorating the life of Jesus are observed. These Sundays remind us of the time between the coming of the Holy Spirit and the return of Christ, the time in which the church is called to carry out the ministry initiated by our Lord. During this time our attention is directed toward the activity of the Holy Spirit in the church, and toward the growth in grace and faith that Christians experience as a result of the Spirit's work. The liturgical color for the Time of the Church is green, symbolizing that growth.

We confess our faith in the church, the communion of saints, the great cloud of witnesses that God has gathered to guide and encourage each believer. Paul addresses all the members of the church as saints; "sainthood" defines our participation in the spiritual growth that the Spirit nurtures in the church. Thus it seems appropriate to call the Time of the Church a "season of saints," a season in which to celebrate the saints who constitute the church and the gifts that confirm us all in our own sainthood.

This months-long celebration of growth and mission is at odds with another "green" seasonal experience of the church: the annual summer slump. The absence of great festivals or holidays from the church calendar between late spring and late autumn makes it difficult for the church to overcome such competing attractions as summer vacations, weekend outings, yard work and ball games, along with a general seasonal aversion to exertion. Many churches cut back their programs in the summer, concentrating their efforts on a week or two of vacation Bible school and an annual outdoor service while deemphasizing regular weekly worship and education ministries. Nearly

9

every congregation assumes that worship attendance will decline over the summer.

Although the church calendar — the concentration of all its festivals in one half of the year, in particular — is partly to blame for the summer slump, one congregation has found in the church calendar a solution to summertime inertia. The church calendar is rich in days that honor memorable people in the history of the faith. All Saints Lutheran Church in Lilburn, Georgia, decided several years ago to observe several of those historical festivals and commemorations during the Time of the Church, using them as occasions to emphasize the gifts and tasks God has given the church and its saints. The response of the worshiping congregation to that year's observances encouraged the worship committee to plan a second series of historical commemorations, and most recently a third. These commemorations counteract the monotony of the long green season, attract the attention of worshipers and continue to elicit enthusiastic response from the members of the congregation.

Each month between Pentecost and All Saints' Day, one or two Sundays' services at All Saints Church are devoted to commemorating exemplary characters in the history of the church. Hymns and prayers for the services are selected according to the significant themes in the lives and careers of the persons being commemorated. Appropriate Scripture readings are also selected, although sometimes the lectionary readings for the Sunday are found suitable; in any case, the special lessons are usually read in addition to the appointed readings rather than in their stead. Each commemoration also includes a sermon that uses the life of the day's honoree to illuminate the life of the church and its saints.

The meditations in this collection were originally prepared for those commemorative worship services. They are lessons in the history of the communion of saints; but more important, they are intended to help today's saints experience the richness of their sainthood. They reflect the context for which they were written, the worship services of a particular congregation.

Thus a few of them speak especially to issues of denominational and congregational identity that may not concern every reader; yet even in those cases they illustrate the devotional use that congregations can make of the lives of the saints.

The commemorations in this series are drawn from the calendar of Lesser Festivals and Commemorations in the *Lutheran Book of Worship.*[1] Congregations that do not have access to that calendar may find similar calendars of saints' days and commemorations in the worship traditions of their own denominations. No "official" calendar, of course, is required; congregations and pastors may want to compile their own list of saints of blessed memory. For the commemorations suggested by the *LBW* valuable additional biographical, bibliographical and worship resources can be found in the *Manual on the Liturgy* and *Festivals and Commemorations,* both by Philip Pfatteicher.[2]

May 24
Nicolaus Copernicus, Teacher, 1542

Facts Complement Faith
Psalm 8

One day last week I ran into a graduate student colleague of mine in the university library. He asked me what I was doing research on, and I told him "Nicolaus Copernicus." That surprised him, since my field is 19th century American Christianity, and Copernicus was a 16th century Polish astronomer. So I explained to him that I was working on a sermon commemorating Copernicus. That surprised him even more. "Why," he wondered, "is a Lutheran church commemorating a Polish Catholic scientist, especially one who is often considered a symbol of the tension between religion and science?"

The easy answer to his question would have been, "Because it says so on our church calendar." But why is Copernicus on our calendar? Sure, we want to honor people of a variety of nationalities, whose contributions to Christian life have been made in a variety of fields. But why is the only day on our calendar commemorating a scientist devoted to Copernicus?

The calendar designates May 24 as the commemoration of "Nicolaus Copernicus, Teacher." That in itself is puzzling. Copernicus was never a teacher. He was a church bureaucrat in a Polish town called Frauenburg, and was trained in medicine, mathematics, astronomy and economics. He wrote two books in his life, one on monetary policy and one on astronomy. He only taught one student in his life, a Lutheran professor from Luther's own university in Wittenberg who traveled to Frauenburg to investigate Copernicus' theories about the solar system.

So if Copernicus is considered a teacher of the church, it's not because he was a classroom whiz. But Copernicus was a teacher in a much broader sense: he taught the whole world new ways of thinking and understanding the universe, so profound that they are often collectively described as the "Copernican revolution."

Copernicus, whose Polish name was Miklaj Kopperningk, was born in 1473, ten years before Martin Luther, and 19 years before Christopher Columbus sailed to the New World. Through the efforts of a clergyman uncle, he was appointed as a young man to a position in church administration, which provided him with a livelihood and an opportunity to study with some of the best teachers in Europe. His special love was mathematics, and he was fascinated by the complex mathematical theories that had been developed since ancient times to explain and predict the movement of heavenly bodies.

Those theories were so complex because they all started with the assumption that the earth is the center of the universe and all the celestial bodies travel around the earth. Of course, that's the way it appears to common sense and the naked eye, and people in a more primitive age had no reason to believe it wasn't so. As more and more data were collected about astronomical events and patterns, it became harder to fit the facts to the theory. For example, sometimes planets seemed to back up, or to exchange positions in the sky. So the mathematical solutions to astronomical puzzles became hopelessly complex.

Even some ancient Greeks had suggested that the sun, rather than the earth, is the center of the planetary system, and the earth travels around the sun along with the planets and comets. Copernicus, aware of those ancient and generally rejected theories, made the bold claim that the hypothesis of a heliocentric universe — one with the sun at the center — made it much simpler to explain the odd behavior of stars and planets. When a planet appeared to move backwards, that planet was moving the same direction as the earth, but slower. When planets switched positions relative to each other, it was because the earth had moved to a point in its orbit that changed the angle at which we viewed the planets.

Years of study convinced Copernicus that this was the true configuration of the universe. He wrote up his findings in a book that remained unpublished for years; Copernicus first saw the published edition of his work on the day of his death, May 24, 1543.

Of course, his theory still had rough edges, and it wasn't until the invention of the telescope and the research of Johannes Kepler and Galileo Galilei a century later that his conclusions were proven valid. But Copernicus had turned the universe on its head, and had begun a revolution in both scientific and religious thought.

Still, many scientists have made important discoveries. Why do we single out Copernicus as a teacher? First, he taught the world a new way of thinking. Medieval people called science "philosophy," and it was. Instead of forming ideas based on facts, people before modern times formed their ideas first about how things should be, and then made the facts fit their ideas.

The combination of Aristotelian philosophy and Christian theology that the Catholic Church stamped with its authority led to a belief that the universe was a certain way, and people bent, looped and carved up their facts to fit the theory.

Copernicus reasoned the other way around: find out the facts and then form a hypothesis that reasonably accounts for the facts. One intense debate provoked by Copernicus' work was whether a hypothesis formed in that way could be considered an attempt at stating the truth. Of course, to question the legitimacy of making up your mind about something after you have the facts instead of before seems ridiculous to modern people, but 450 years ago that was an astonishing breakthrough. It's easy to see how we moderns are beneficiaries of the Copernican revolution.

What Copernicus did in astronomy is similar to what Martin Luther was doing at the same time in theology. In fact, Copernicus has been called the "Luther of science," and Luther has been called the "Copernicus of theology." Copernicus refused to accept a system of astronomy that contradicted mathematics, and Luther refused to accept a system of theology that contradicted the Bible. Each man claimed the right to form his own conclusions based on original information, and each one revolutionized his own discipline. They never convinced each other: Copernicus remained a loyal Catholic and Luther called Copernicus a "fool who would upset the art of astronomy," but they made parallel movements of mind and spirit.

But that still doesn't establish Copernicus' significance for the modern church. What did the Copernican revolution contribute to Christian thought? On one hand, a problem. The ancient view — that the sun, stars and planets revolve around the earth — is reflected in much of the language in the Bible. If Copernicus is right, the Bible is wrong; if the Bible is right, Copernicus is wrong. But there's a third way of relating the two positions: both Copernicus and the Bible are right, and the disagreement only results from a wrong interpretation of the Bible.

In the Bible, God reveals himself to inspire our faith and guide our conduct. The center of the revelation is God's grace in Jesus Christ. But God chose to communicate his revelation through the writings of an assortment of human authors over hundreds of years, and as human beings they expressed their faith in the language and concepts of their own time. The language and the worldview might change, but the revelation still remains valid. So, although the writers of the Bible proclaimed

God to be the creator of a universe with the earth at its center, changing the details of the picture doesn't change the truth of the revelation: Copernicus moved the pieces around, but still confessed that God had created them.

Three hundred years after Copernicus, a new battle between science and faith erupted over Charles Darwin's theory of evolution. Again, changing the details of the story doesn't necessarily change the point of the story, and many Christians have no trouble believing that God created us even if it took much longer than people used to believe. But Darwin went further: his theory includes the principle of random mutations and natural selection of the fittest. It specifically denies any loving purpose, any guiding principle, any Creator or sustainer or provider. Darwin challenged the meaning of the creation story for Christian faith: Copernicus challenged the terms in which the story is told.

Aside from challenging our way of thinking, Copernicus' theory made some positive contributions to Christian thought. It vastly enlarged our sense of the size of God's creation. One objection to his theory was that the stars don't seem to change their relative position in the sky: if the earth is moving around, why doesn't the angle or distance between stars seem to change? Copernicus speculated that the stars are so far away the few million miles the earth moves in a year don't make any difference discernible by the naked eye. The later invention of the telescope affirmed his theory.

That information made the scope of God's creation and providence millions of times greater than human beings had ever imagined. God hadn't just created a little greenhouse earth with a lighted sky-dome over it that he could sit in heaven and keep an eye on: he had created a universe that stretched for billions of miles, with movement and order and precision and balance and beauty that served no apparent purpose but his own pleasure in it.

Which in turn makes God's grace the more amazing. If the earth is the center of the universe and human beings are the most important creatures on it, then it only makes sense for God to be supremely concerned about us. But if we are tiny specks on a little piece of dust in the corner of an infinite cosmos, then for God to tend to us day-by-day and to have sent his own Son to die for us can only be considered astonishingly gracious acts of love.

Copernicus believed all that. He never thought his book, *On the Revolution of Celestial Orbs,* could undermine Christian faith. In fact, he loved to study the skies because it added to his wonder at the greatness and grace of God. In an age when it has become customary to hold the claims of science and of faith in tension, we do well to learn from Nicolaus Copernicus, teacher: to learn that the insights of science complement our confession of faith; to learn to desire knowledge and understanding of the universe God has created. Amen.

June 14
Basil the Great, Bishop of Caesarea, 379
Gregory of Nazianzus, Bishop of Constantinople, c. 389
Gregory, Bishop of Nyssa, c. 385

The Cappadocian Fathers
Colossians 2:1-7

Today we're commemorating three Greek theologians of the fourth century: Basil of Caesarea, Gregory of Nazianzus and Gregory of Nyssa. None of the three is likely to be familiar to Christians today. Basil and Gregory and Gregory are often called the Three Great Cappadocian Fathers. But their title is unlikely to mean anything to most of us, either. These three men are not household names. So today might be a "so what?" day in our church calendar, when we say, "What is so important about three bishops who lived in Asia Minor 1,600 years ago, and why do we devote a Sunday morning of worship to remembering them?"

I'd like to mention two things in particular that are important about the Cappadocian Fathers: two things they represent in the history of the church that we do well to be reminded of today. But first, let me just tell you who they were.

19

Basil of Caesarea and Gregory of Nyssa were brothers and Gregory of Nazianzus was their close friend. They were natives of the region of Asia Minor called Cappadocia and they all came from prominent Christian families: in fact, Basil and Gregory's sister, both parents and all four grandparents became saints. All three of our honorees were wealthy, well-educated and cultured, but they gave up their promising public careers and their fortunes to enter a monastery. All three eventually became bishops and important theologians.

The most important thing we remember about the three Cappadocian Fathers is their contribution to Christian doctrine. They were active at a time when the great doctrines of the church were just being developed through long and intense debate. Basil and his brother and friend played leading parts in defining the true Christian teaching, especially concerning the Trinity. Some of the issues they debated sound obscure to us today, but in the fourth century, Christian orthodoxy hung in the balance and the abilities of bishops like Basil and the two Gregorys to define terms carefully and precisely allowed the Christian faith to develop and survive in the form we hold today. For example, when we say that the Trinity is one God in three persons, we confess a belief the Cappadocians helped preserve and explain. They defended the idea that God the Son and God the Holy Spirit are coeternal with the Father, against opponents who claimed God the Father created God the Son and the Holy Spirit later, and that therefore the Son and the Holy Spirit are separate and secondary Gods. The debates over these questions were bitter and intense, and often involved the Roman emperors themselves, and the bishops who defended the orthodox faith did so at great personal risk.

The memory of these men and their struggle to defend the faith reminds us that what we believe is important. That's easy for us to forget in our age of religious toleration and pluralism. Many people seem convinced that "It doesn't matter what you believe, as long as you're sincere," and "It's not what you believe, but how you live your life." Now, toleration is a great achievement of modern religion, and we're rightly thankful that Christians don't slaughter one another over fine points of doctrine anymore; but what we believe still matters. We confess that Jesus is the Truth, and therefore knowing what the truth is, is a matter of life and death to us.

The Cappadocian Fathers' theological writings show us something else, as well. Christianity has a credibility problem in the modern world. Things that can't be proven or documented by credible scientific evidence don't carry much weight in our world anymore. Many people regard all religion and belief in the supernatural as ancient mythology.

That problem was around in the fourth century, too. The Cappadocians lived in the world of the great Greek philosophers, the masters of wisdom. In that world, a religion that worshiped a man who was also God, who was born in a barn and executed as a rabble-rouser, was ridiculed. And when Christians started talking about their one God who appeared to be three Gods, or three persons of God who were actually one being, they were hooted at. But Basil and the two Gregorys expressed Christian beliefs in a way that was intellectually respectable. In fact, far from being beneath the intellectual abilities of the scoffers, the puzzling aspects of Christian theology actually are far beyond people's ability to understand. When Christians accept great mysteries by faith, we're not being foolish; we're acknowledging a wisdom far beyond our grasp.

Besides their theological contributions, the Cappadocian Fathers played a major role in showing how Christians ought to live in the world. They lived in a difficult time for Christians. Until 20 years before these three men were born, Christianity was illegal in the Roman Empire, and no one was a Christian who wasn't absolutely committed to Christ and willing to die for their faith.

But beginning in the year 312, Christianity was first legalized and then made the official religion of the Empire. Suddenly the masses of people considered themselves Christians, whether or not they really cared about religion. The Sunday-morning Christian was born, along with the Christmas-and-

Easter Christian and the socially-correct Christian. People who were serious about trying to live out their faith in true devotion felt out of place in the church, and many, like the Cappadocian Fathers, went to live in monasteries as full-time practitioners of intense discipleship.

Again, it isn't hard to see the parallel in our own time. Christianity is practically woven into the fabric of our American culture, and for that reason it is often absent from our culture. Because we think of America as a Christian nation, many people think all there is to being a Christian is to be a good citizen, a nice guy, a good father or mother, perhaps a church member. In recent years, calling oneself a born-again Christian has become a status-badge in certain political circles.

But being part of a Christian culture robs Christianity of its central significance. Paul wrote that being a Christian means being crucified to the world and everything in it, and living only to God. Christianity as a way of thinking, living and believing, is incompatible with any strictly human or worldly value. And that's what Basil and his family and friends believed was at stake in a Christian society: if Christianity becomes completely identified with nation, society or world, then the only way for Christians to deny the world is to leave it. So they went to the monasteries.

But they didn't just go to the monasteries to avoid getting tangled up with the world. The monastic life was a life rich in devotion, prayer, study and contemplation. It was in the hours of prayer and meditation they spent in the monastery that these men developed their great theologial statements. And it was in prayer, fasting and worship in their retreats far away from the everyday world that they were strengthened to lead the church through its difficult days.

Christians need that kind of spiritual refreshment. The gospels tell us that Jesus often went off by himself to pray: onto a mountain top, or out on a lake in a boat or into the Garden of Gethsemane. One book suggests that a commemoration of the Cappadocian Fathers should include prayers for "pastors who long for time for prayer and contemplation."[3]

It's something most pastors don't have enough of, but pastors aren't unique in that regard. All Christians can be strengthened and sustained spiritually by spending time every day in devotion, prayer and Scripture reading.

And though they became monks, Basil and the two Gregorys were never preoccupied with their own private spiritual lives. Instead, they devoted their lives to serving both the church and the world. Basil became the chief bishop of all Asia Minor and fought to preserve the church from the meddling of the civil authorities and from internal strife and schism. The two Gregorys led their own churches through conflicts and controversies and continued Basil's work after he died. And their charity and service extended beyond the church, into the community around them. During a famine several years before Basil became a bishop, he sold all his extensive personal property for the benefit of the starving. And as a bishop, he organized charities and relief work, forbidding Christians under his authority from discriminating against non-Christians in their aid to the needy. When he died in January of 379, he was mourned by the entire city of Caesarea — Jews, Christians and pagans alike.

Basil and the other Cappadocian Fathers set us an example of the balanced Christian life that comes close to the biblical ideal. It seems almost impossible for most of us to give proper attention to our own spiritual well-being, our shared life with other Christians and our service to the world beyond the church. Most Christians, and most churches, emphasize one of those at the expense of the others. But the complete Christian life is all those things, and the three giants of the church that we commemorate today can be models for us of such a life.

One day's commemoration will probably not make Basil, Gregory and Gregory anyone's personal heroes. But whether or not the Cappadocians become familiar names in our household, the faith you confess today and the life you lead as a Christian today are shaped by their influence. And their example reminds us of what it means to be Christians in the circumstances in which we live. Amen.

23

June 25
Presentation of the Augsburg Confession, 1530
Philipp Melanchthon, Renewer of the Church, 1560

Unity and Particularity:
Our Confession Of Faith
Romans 3:21-28

The Augsburg Confession is the definitive confession of faith of the Lutheran church. Among all Christian writings, Lutherans rank the Augsburg Confession third, behind only the Scriptures and the Creeds. All Lutherans in the world recognize the Augsburg Confession as the guide to their faith. You might be surprised to learn that all Lutherans in the world agree on anything, but we do. All the many differences we exhibit are within the bounds of a faith shaped by the Augsburg Confession.

You might also be surprised to learn that the universal, definitive statement of what Lutherans believe was not written by Martin Luther, but by someone named Philipp Melanchthon. To explain Melanchthon's authorship, and the reason for the Augsburg Confession's importance among Lutherans, we can review the events that led to the writing of the Confession.

The Reformation is said to have begun when Luther published his Ninety-five Theses in the year 1517. People had objected to abuses and errors in the Catholic Church before that, but they had usually been silenced or forced to recant. Luther's unprecedented success in raising the cry for reform was partly due to the political situation in Europe at the time. Rival powers were struggling for control of the Holy Roman Empire and the German states were beginning to move toward independence. So when the Pope and the Catholic magistrates excommunicated and condemned Luther, some of the German princes found it to their political advantage to protect him, and to defend his beliefs. People in those princes' territories enthusiastically accepted Luther's ideas and the Pope and the Emperor were powerless to quench the reforming spirit.

Not until 1530 did the political situation stabilize enough for the religious controversy to be settled, but by then the new views had spread throughout Germany and other protest movements had begun in Switzerland and elsewhere. To address the religious problem, the Emperor called a council of the empire and the church to meet at Augsburg and invited the Lutherans to prepare a statement of their doctrines for othe council to study. The statement of faith adopted by the Lutherans was presented at Augsburg on June 25, 1530, and is known to us as the Augsburg Confession.

Why didn't Luther write it himself? Since he had been excommunicated and condemned, the princes who were protecting him couldn't guarantee his safety if he ventured outside their territory to go to Augsburg. Also, Luther wasn't cut out for debating. He was hot-tempered and emotional, quick to lash out at his opponents, prone to exaggerate his ideas to make a point. His close friend and fellow reformer, Melanchthon, was a careful scholar, much more inclined to seek common ground and work for an agreement than to attack his opponents. So with Luther's blessing, Melanchthon wrote the

Augsburg Confession and defended it at the Imperial Diet. Although Luther didn't write the Confession, Melanchthon was such a close friend and ardent follower of Luther the ideas in the Confession can be considered Luther's own.

But that story is now more than 450 years old. The political intrigues and religious conflicts of the Reformation are matters for history books. Of what significance is the Augsburg Confession to Lutheran Christians today?

First, the Augsburg Confession is a document of Christian unity. That's another surprise, since it's the distinctive statement of Lutheran beliefs. But Melanchthon's purpose in writing it was not to draw the line between Lutherans and other Christians. He was trying to present the beliefs of the Lutherans in a way that would win the approval of the Emperor and his counselors, to show that the Lutheran doctrine was also true Christian doctrine. Basing his arguments on Scripture and the teachings of the earliest Christians, he outlined a vision of the gospel that he hoped would unite Christians in common confession. The Lutheran movement was never intended to divide the church, but to unite the church in a new level of trust in God's promises.

Sadly, the Council rejected Melanchthon's proposal, and it wasn't long before the Lutherans themselves came to see their doctrines as a way of distinguishing themselves from other Christians. From that time until recently, Christian history has been a history of seeking distinctions and differences rather than unity. But the original spirit of Lutheran Christianity was a spirit of unity, of finding a way to express the Christian faith that would gather all Christians into a loving, trusting, family of God.

Significantly, as the relationship between Lutherans and Roman Catholics has improved in recent years, the Augsburg Confession has been the doctrinal basis for our newfound agreement. Catholics have recognized that much of the Confession does proclaim the Christian faith as they understand it; and Lutherans have rediscovered that the Augsburg Confession was created as a document of Christian unity rather than division.

The second witness the Augsburg Confession makes in the 20th century church is to the importance of a particular way of believing. The Confession is a statement of particular understanding of the Christian faith, an understanding that has always been the essential mark of Lutheranism. The Lutheran church is called a confessional church, because it is a particular confession of faith that defines what is Lutheran. Except for conservative Presbyterians and some Mennonites, no other major denomination is defined by a specific statement of what it believes. Other Christian denominations are distinguished by their forms of church organization, their way of interpreting the Bible, their manner of administering baptism, their requirements for church membership, their description of Christian conversion or some other feature.

Lutheranism's standing as a great world religious body is a result of one thing: our commitment to a specific confession of faith. The thing we offer the world that no other denomination offers is a consistent, concise and distinctive declaration of what Lutheran Christians believe. That's the reason Lutherans put such a great emphasis on doctrine: apart from our confessional heritage being Lutheran means nothing.

And that's more important now than ever for Lutherans in this country. For three centuries, being Lutherans in America has been largely a cultural and ethnic identity: you were a Lutheran if your ancestors came from Denmark or Norway or Saxony; you were a Lutheran if you ate lutefisk at Christmas or sang *Stille Nacht* in German; you were a Lutheran if you lived in Minnesota and loved coffee or in Wisconsin and loved beer.

But now the old identities ae fading, and we're becoming more inclusive and more American. Consequently, if Lutheran identity is to mean anything at all in this country, it must be defined by what we believe, not where our grandparents came from. The Lutheran church has emerged from its ethnic ghettoes over the last 50 years to become a major national denomination, but we have yet to make the American public aware of what we offer. We have declared our intention to reach out to refugees and members of minority groups as well as to the American population as a whole, but people outside the traditional Lutheran constituency will not be attracted to a church that still defines itself by the ethnic customs of past generations. Without our confession of faith, our existence as a denomination is hardly justified — or likely to continue.

The third reason for remembering the Augsburg Confession is the most important: the content of the Confession. What is the theological vision that sustains the Lutheran church? Simply stated, it's the phrase most of us remember from confirmation class: justification by grace alone through faith alone. Our Confession states that all human beings and all human activities are captive to sin. But God freely forgives sinners, accepts us as righteous and gives us eternal life as an outright gift for the sake of Jesus Christ. This salvation by God's free grace can only be received by faith: we can't earn it, deserve it or achieve it. And the faith by which we receive salvation is itself a gift from God. God puts faith in our hearts by the work of the Holy Spirit, through the preached word and the sacraments of Baptism and Communion. And the gifts of faith and grace create a new life in us, make us new persons who are sons and daughters of God and members of the church. The acts of service and love that constitute the Christian life are the natural result of what God has done in our lives.

Thus the Confession of faith that defines Lutheran Christianity is entirely focused on God and his loving actions for us. God is for us; he gave his Son's life for us; and he gives himself to us in his word and his body and blood. Our understanding of the church, the ordained ministry, the sacraments, the Bible and the Christian life is based on our belief that every significant act in the drama of our salvation is done entirely by God out of his own free and limitless love. The measureless love of God, always acting for our benefit through Jesus Christ, is the center of the Lutheran faith. The life we live in response to that grace can take a variety of shapes, but it is always a life of simple trust in the absolute love of God.

That's the Augsburg Confession — that's Lutheranism — in a paragraph. That's what we're commemorating today. And that's what we as a church and a denomination offer the world as our hope and promise. And if there is a uniqueness to our confessional heritage, it's not a way for us to set ourselves apart from other Christians, but a place for us to stand as we join with other Christians in proclaiming Christ to the world. Amen.

July 11
Benedict of Nursia, Ábbot of Monte Cassino, c. 540

Christianity And Culture
John 17:14-18

Today we're commemorating Benedict of Nursia. Benedict is another of those historical characters that modern Christians may have heard of, but who is at best only a name to most of us. Most of us have probably heard of Saint Benedict only if we've lived near a church or a college named for him, or toured a Benedictine abbey. So who was Benedict and why is he on our calendar of commemorations?

Benedict was one of those people — Martin Luther and Mahatma Gandhi were others — who changed the course of history without really intending to, simply because their personalities and their convictions perfectly matched the needs of the age in which they lived. He lived at the height, or the depth, of a great crisis in our world history. And although he was only looking for a way to escape the turmoil and anxiety, he inadvertently helped determine the outcome of the crisis.

Benedict was born in the Italian town of Nursia sometime around the year 480. The final collapse of the Roman Empire had occurred just four years earlier when a barbarian chief named Odoacer had overthrown the emperor. The classic civilization of Ancient Rome was in ruins, and the uncivilized barbarians reigned over Europe. The psychological state of the once-great Romans was something like the mood of American Southerners after the Civil War. Their way of life had collapsed; their cities and buildings were rubble; their great noble families had become servants of a foreign army; everything they had always had faith in had failed them — including Christianity, which had been the official religion of Rome for about 170 years.

To young Benedict, it seemed like the only way to survive the catastrophe was to escape it by becoming a religious hermit. So when he was about 20 years old he joined a monastery. He was too serious about his religious life to be popular with the lackadaisical monks in that place, so he left and in the year 529 founded his own monastery at a place called Monte Cassino.

Over the years his quiet, disciplined practice of the Christian life attracted other monks to Monte Cassino, and eventually Benedict wrote a Rule — a guide to Christian life — for monks. Benedict died around the year 540, and after his death, monks from Monte Cassino began to move all over Europe and to establish new monasteries that followed the Benedictine Rule. The Benedictines became the mightiest force in spreading Christianity among the barbarians and Christianizing Europe, and they were also the most important preservers of classical culture and learning through the so-called "Dark Ages." The religious and cultural influence of the Benedictines has led one historian to assert that Benedict was largely responsible for the shape of European civilization — an amazing assessment of a man who was only looking for peace of mind and a quiet place to pray.[4]

What in particular did Benedict create with his Rule and his monastery that is of enduring significance? First, he started a movement that encouraged simple Christian living. There had been monks for at least a couple of hundred years by Benedict's time, but they had often practiced an extreme form of self-denial and heroic discipline. They lived by themselves in caves and fasted for years at a time, for example, or tried to stop practicing such decadent worldly luxuries as sleeping.

Benedict's version of the Christian life didn't require super-heroic efforts at holiness, but simple day-to-day dedication. His rule required his monks to do four things: pray throughout the day; worship eight times each day; study the Scriptures; and do useful labor. The Benedictine monks were also required to live in a community with other monks, and to be completely obedient to the abbot of the monastery.

Benedictine monasticism has gotten a bad reputation in modern times. In the late Middle Ages, the monks were criticized by Dominican and Franciscan friars, who traveled all over the world preaching the gospel and doing acts of charity. To the activist friars, the monks living in their monasteries were escapists, who fled the world instead of trying to save it. Later, Martin Luther and other Protestants claimed that monasteries were places where people tried to save themselves through holy living instead of trusting God's grace to save them, and monasteries were abolished in the Protestant countries of Europe.

These later criticisms notwithstanding, Benedict and his movement were the perfect answer to the needs of their times. They might have overemphasized certain aspects of their religion, but in the chaos of the Fall of Rome when it was just as likely that Christianity would become barbarianized as that the barbarians would become Christianized, perhaps nothing could have preserved the Christian heritage other than groups of Christians who renounced the world, withdrew from the fray and spent their time in prayer, worship and study. And when the Benedictines began spreading across Europe and planting Christianity in hostile barbarian lands, it was the depth and stability of their devotional life that made it possible for them to survive and attract converts.

We need to remember their example today. Modern Christians are heirs to the activist tradition of the friars who tried to save the world and to the theological tradition of the Protestants, and we tend to forget the importance of the kind of spirituality the monks practiced. The Rule of Saint Benedict encouraged frequent prayers, regular worship, Scripture study, community of believers and Christian obedience, and we need that kind of spiritual foundation for whatever else we want to do as Christians in the world. In recent years, as Protestants have begun to realize that we lack spiritual depth, many Protestant pastors and educators have turned to the Benedictines for direction: the Benedictine Abbey at Collegeville, Minnesota, has attained worldwide importance as a retreat center for Protestants as well as Catholics; and many of the contemporary worship resources we use were developed by the Order of Saint Benedict.

On the other hand, while the Benedictines were retreating from the confusion of the crumbling Roman world, they were also preserving the best of their culture. Benedict encouraged monks to copy ancient manuscripts — not because he thought scholarship was important, but because he wanted to keep the monks busy so they could avoid temptation. Copying old books was purely busy work. But all those copies of old works that piled up in monastery attics became the repository of classical literature in the Middle Ages. And though scholarship was not especially valued by Benedict, the monks and nuns of the Benedictine order eventually became known as learned scholars and teachers.

Benedict's order also preserved much of the Roman outlook. Benedict was a Roman nobleman, and the Rule he wrote for his order embodied the same discipline, order, obedience and organization that had distinguished Roman law and government. Though the Roman Empire was dying, much of its spirit lived on in the Benedictine order, and as the Benedictines spread Christianity through barbarian Europe, they also unwittingly spread the Roman sense of law and social order. So while the monks and nuns of Saint Benedict were withdrawing from the society around them, they were also distilling and preserving its culture, its art and its way of thinking.

Benedict reminds us of the two-sided relationship Christians have with the world. We are not part of the world: we don't really belong here, or derive our strength, our hope or our value from the society or the nation we live in. But at the same time, it's impossible to separate ourselves from the world. We always participate in the life of the community we live in. So we need to be aware of how our culture influences our religious values, and how we as Christians can shape our culture. Much of what Benedict believed was common-sense Christianity was really part of his Roman heritage. In the same way, some of what we consider basic Christian values are really American political values, modern scientific assumptions or prejudices of one form or another. It's especially important when we share our faith with people of other nations and cultures that we're not confusing it with nationalism and just trying to make Americans out of the people we encounter.

At the same time, we need to be aware of the way we can influence culture. Benedict and his followers preserved the best of classical literature, art and social organization and bequeathed it to European civilization. In our churches, our church colleges and schools, and our homes we do the same thing. We have the responsibility, and the power, to influence what our culture finds beautiful and valuable, and to guide our civilization in the way it uses knowledge.

"In the world but not of the world," is the way the Bible describes the status of Christians: Benedict and the monks of Monte Cassino illustrate that relationship. When Jesus sent his disciples out to spread the news of his kingdom, he sent them like "lambs among wolves (Luke 10:3)." In that precarious balance of alienation from the world and responsibility for the world, we do well to remember the example of the Benedictines, who used spiritual discipline to strengthen their faith and protect them from the hostility of the world even while they were changing the world. Amen.

July 15
Vladimir, First Christian Ruler of Russia, 1015
Olga, Confessor, 969

"The Devil Was Overcome By Fools And Madmen"
Romans 7:4-6

Vladimir of Kiev is known as the Apostle to the Russians. It was under his rule that Christianity became the major religion in what was eventually known as Russia: thus Vladimir is to Russia what Saint Patrick is to Ireland and Saint Olaf is to Norway. 1988 marked the one thousandth anniversary of Vladimir's conversion, which is also celebrated as the formal birthday of the Russian Orthodox Church.

The biographer who recorded the story of Saint Vladimir for later generations summed up his life this way: "The Devil was overcome by fools and madmen."[5] That's a peculiar thing to say about your patron saint, but Vladimir was a peculiar saint. He was the Grand Duke of Kiev, when Kiev was the most powerful city in a nation still mostly made up of bloodthirsty barbarians and idol-worshipers. As the Grand Duke, Vladimir was the head bloodthirsty barbarian. His biographer commented that Vladimir's "desire for women was too much for him," and that he had numerous wives and even more numerous female slaves.[6] He was also a brutal warrior and ruler, infamous for murder and treachery. But, then, brutality ran in Vladimir's family: his grandmother, Olga, who also eventually became a saint, avenged her husband's assassination by cooking his assassins in hot steam, and then plotted the murder of hundreds of their followers.

Surrounded by Christian empires, however, and seeing the example of his grandmother who had died a Christian, Vladimir decided at about age 30 that he should become a Christian, too, though his reason seems to have been more political than spiritual. Resolved to become a Christian, he went to war against the Byzantine Empire to force the Greek Orthodox Church to baptize him and accept him as a member. When that didn't work, he went to war as an ally of the Byzantine Emperor, and forced the emperor to give Vladimir his sister as a bride; and then for her sake the Emperor ordered that Vladimir be baptized.

No convert was ever more zealous for his new religion than Vladimir was. He summoned missionaries to Russia, and set out to do away with idol worship. When preaching and persuasion didn't work, he sent soldiers to smash idols and destroy pagan temples. And those same soldiers herded people by the thousands into the River Dnieper at sword point and forced them to be baptized.

Vladimir sent away all his wives and mistresses except his new Christian wife, and made every effort to practice the discipline of his new faith. He became deeply penitent over all his excesses and abuses of power: he worried that as a Christian ruler he should no longer use force against his enemies, or even authorize the punishment of criminals.

Vladimir died in the year 1015, after ruling 30 years as a Christian prince, and after finally giving away all his personal belongings to his Christian friends and to the poor people of Kiev.

A peculiar saint. What are we to think of someone who begins as a torturer, goes to war and carries off a princess to force the church to baptize him, converts his people by force, and finally becomes a kindly, generous old man? Why do we celebrate a man like that 1,000 years later?

Then again, maybe Vladimir isn't such a peculiar saint. In fact, maybe a saint like Vladimir is more real than the saints we usually picture with folded hands and pious faces, the saints who never did wrong or embarrassed their families or put their feet in their mouths. Look at Vladimir, trying to be a good ruler and to find a satisfying religious orientation for his life; stumbling over his own enthusiasm and his own slightly skewed personality; but still trying, and remaining faithful to the end. Who does Vladimir remind you of?

He reminds me of Moses, who killed a man, disobeyed God, lost his temper and broke the tablets of the law, but never stopped believing the promise and rallying of the Israelites. He reminds me of David, the shining King of Israel, who also couldn't control his desire for women, and suffered terribly for it; but who was still the head of the line from which Jesus was born.

Vladimir reminds me of Peter, the disciple who loved Jesus most dearly and misunderstood him most completely, who disobeyed and denied Jesus, and still became the rock of the church. He reminds me of Martin Luther, whose hot temper and intolerance of people who disagreed with him made him as many enemies as his tender and devout preaching won him followers.

But most of all, Vladimir reminds me of me, and the people I know best. For all our good intentions, we always have to wonder if our motives are pure, or whether we're trying to be Christians for our own benefit. And beyond motives and intentions, the lists of our failings and fallings would fill books, and our successes would barely make a footnote.

Yet we struggle on, against our own temptations and weaknesses, against the workings of an institutional church that often seems like a bad practical joke, against a world that is hostile to Christ and his purposes. And while his army of misfits stumbles and wanders along, God is patient with us, and forgives us, and leads us back when we go the wrong direction. And we have every confidence that, like Vladimir, we'll come out in the right place. We cling to the hope that we'll be loving and faithful people, and that our efforts will advance the church in its work.

"The Devil was overcome by fools and madmen." This extravagant, impulsive Grand Duke of Kiev, who reached for his sword when he should have reached for his Bible, planted the Christian church in Russian soil, where it took root and flourished. And though he may never have been troubled by the finer points of etiquette or Christian doctrine, his faithfulness and commitment never faltered. His repentance, his gratitude to God for his salvation and his devotion to his duty as he understood it were sincere and simple; and it is for the simplicity and sincerity of his faith that we remember him more than for anything else.

That simple, childlike faith is too often treated scornfully by Christians, especially in mainline churches that have traditions to protect. We're proud of our doctrines and our liturgies, and we're tempted to look down on people who celebrate their experience of God's power in less sophisticated ways. And we're embarrassed by someone like Vladimir, who got carried away by the sheer joy of his conversion, and ran off to serve God if it killed him and everybody else in Kiev, by God! — and is remembered today as a great saint.

Martin Luther is often quoted as having said "Sin boldly," and the advice sounds shocking. But when Luther said "Sin boldly," he was talking about a situation like Vladimir's. He observed that many Christians are so worried they'll say or do the wrong thing that they never say or do anything at all. But because we have the promise of forgiveness by God's grace, we're free from that kind of worrying, and we should be bold in our efforts to serve God and to reform the world around us. And if our zeal gets a little bigger than our wisdom and we err, we can turn to God in repentance and he will forgive us.

It's a new twist on Davy Crockett's motto, "Be sure you're right, then go ahead." Because we're all sinners and have only a limited understanding of the truth, and because we live in a sinful and imperfect world, we can never be completely sure we're right. But we must go ahead anyway, trusting that God will forgive us when our boldness causes us to sin.

Finally, our commemoration of Saint Vladimir and 1,000 years of Russian Christianity reminds us of the long Christian tradition of the Russian people. Because the Soviet Union has been dominated for 70 years by a Party that is officially atheist, we're likely to forget that the Russian cultural heritage is Christian 50 generations deep, and that the Christian church is still alive in the Soviet Union. Whatever the philosophy of the Kremlin, the Russian people are historically religious people. We need to remember their tradition of faith if we want to understand them. And we need to remember them as our brothers and sisters in Christ, and pray for their deliverance from religious oppression.

The Lutheran church has in recent years begun dialogue with the Orthodox church in the Soviet Union, and the first agreement we reached was that no matter what system of government we live under, we have a common mission to do whatever is in our power to secure peace and justice for future generations. Today we've discovered that we also have a hero in common: Vladimir, the patron saint of all fools and madmen who would overcome the devil in spite of themselves. Amen.

Bartolomé de Las Casas, Missionary to the Indies, 1566

Padre Of The Americas
Matthew 28:16-20

We are quickly approaching the 500th Anniversary of
Christopher Columbus' "discovery" of the Americas in 1492,
and Spain and nations in the Americas are preparing to observe the anniversary. The celebration in 1992 will include a
World's Fair in Seville and the Olympics in Barcelona. That
anniversary is a proper context for today's commemoration
of Bartolomé de Las Casas, a pioneer Spanish colonist and
an early missionary in the New World. Las Casas is sometimes
called the Padre of the Americas and the Apostle to the Indians.

The 500th anniversary is being observed with a certain sense
of irony. Many Latin Americans, African Americans and
American Indians are taking this opportunity to remind us that
the coming of Europeans to America meant centuries of violence and oppression to most non-Europeans. And that's part
of the story of Bartolomé de Las Casas, too. He was at one

time a slave-owner and oppressor, but later became the leading defender of the Indians in Central America.

When Columbus returned to Spain from the Caribbean, the significance of his discovery was immediately obvious to his king and queen. He told them of a whole new world, of land and minerals and nations of culturally unadvanced inhabitants. Several things were apparent to the Spaniards: first, they had an opportunity on the new continent to create an empire that would vault Spain to the top of the heap of world powers. Second, the gold and treasure in those new lands could finance the expansion of Spanish power. Third, other nations would be quick to challenge Spain's supremacy in the New World.

Fourth, the natives of the Americas needed to hear the gospel. The opportunity to make Christians of the Indians was important to the pious rulers of Spain, and became even more important after the Protestant rebellion began around 1520. Still, the religious motive for conquering the New World never overshadowed the desire for wealth and power. A soldier who accompanied Hernando Cortés on his conquest of Mexico wrote in his memoirs, "We came to serve God and the King, and also to get rich."[7]

The Spaniards developed a system that would accomplish all their objectives. It was called the *encomienda,* in which a colonist was granted a piece of land in America and the labor of all the natives living on it. In return he assumed the obligation of protecting the Indians on his land and instructing them in the Christian faith. With *encomiendas* spread through the colonies, the Spaniards' claims to the land were secured, they had a reliable way to harvest its wealth and the Indians were brought in contact with the teachings of the church.

In theory, at least, the *encomienda* system was like the feudal system of the Middle Ages in Europe, in which serfs lived on land owned by a baron and turned their crops over to him in return for his protection and a place to live. In practice, though, it was more like slavery. *Encomenderos* treated their Indian wards brutally; *conquistadores* waged ruthless wars to bring more and more natives under the control of the Spanish crown; and they justified the subjugation by the necessity of preaching Christ to the pagans.

This was the situation in which Bartolomé de Las Casas raised his voice in defense of the Indians. In his early life he seemed an unlikely reformer. He was born in 1474, which made him roughly a contemporary of Martin Luther and Nicolaus Copernicus. His father traveled to America on Columbus' second expedition and Las Casas himself became a colonist in Cuba after he graduated from the university in 1502. As an *encomendero,* he heard and rejected the early criticisms of the *encomienda* system.

In about 1512, he was ordained a priest — the first priest ordained in the New World, according to a some sources — and in 1514 he underwent a change in his view of the justice of the Spanish conquest. He was working on a sermon on Ecclesiasticus 34:18, which reads, "If one sacrifices from what has been wrongfully obtained, the offering is blemished; the gifts of the lawless are not acceptable." Las Casas was convinced that the verse condemned the system of *conquistadores* and *encomiendas;* it was wrong to claim religious devotion as an excuse for robbing and enslaving the Indians.

Las Casas quickly began trying to find a better way to settle the colonies and Christianize the Indians. Instead of conquest, slavery and forced conversions, he argued, the Spaniards should use peaceful persuasion and their good example to create communities of Indian farmers, where priests could teach and administer the sacraments. Several of Las Casas' own attempts to create such communities failed. But in the 1530s he went into an area in present-day Nicaragua that was called Tierra de Guerra, "Land of War," because of the constant fierce hostility between the Spaniards and the Indians in the area. Within a few years, he had established a successful mission, and eventually renamed the area Vera Paz: "True Peace."

Las Casas was also an advocate for the native Americans in the Spanish court. His arguments before the authorities in

Spain led to the adoption of laws in 1542 that virtually abolished the *encomienda* system. Governors in the New World had a hard time enforcing the new laws over the objections of *encomenderos*. So in 1544, Las Casas returned to America as the Bishop of Chiapas, in Mexico, where a big part of his job was to promote the humane reforms.

In 1547, at the age of 73, Las Casas returned to Spain, not to retire but to begin a new career as a theologian. He rejected the customary use of Christian theology to justify the conquest of the Americas and the exploitation of Indians. During the days of the Inquisition it was dangerous for anyone to disagree with the official position of the church in Spain. But Las Casas spoke out. In 1551 King Charles V ordered Las Casas to appear before the Council of the Indies to debate a theologian named Sepulveda, a prominent supporter of the conquest. The King even ordered all military conquests in the New World halted pending the outcome of the debate.

Sepulveda's arguments ran like this: the Indians were savages and heathens, and therefore deserved to be punished for their sins; some people are by nature inferior, and must serve their superiors; and the spread of Christianity was so important that any means to accomplish it were justified. Las Casas rejected all of Sepulveda's defenses of the conquest. "All peoples of the world are men [i.e., human beings]," he asserted.[8] All people have equal capacity for noble, rational and moral thinking; all deserve respect. There are no naturally superior races or nations. And at no time have Christians been given the authority to convert other people by abusing them. People can only be won over to the Christian faith with "love and gentleness and kindness."[9]

Las Casas' debate with Sepulveda seems to have ended in a draw. The conquest of the Americas was resumed, but with new restraint: Sepulveda's rationalization of racism and oppression was discredited. Las Casas continued to write and speak in the Indians' cause for another 15 years until his death in 1566 just short of his 92nd birthday.

What does the life of Bartolomé de Las Casas mean for us as we approach the 500th anniversary of Europeans in America? First, it reminds us of the sad history of cultural and racial conflict in this hemisphere. Much of Latin America is still shaken by political and economical upheaval, a direct legacy of centuries of exploitation by the colonizers.

When Nelson Mandela visited the United States in 1990, the South African reformer pledged his support to Native Americans in their pursuit of justice, reminding us that our own history in this country is not innocent of oppression. The colonists and pioneers in North America treated the native inhabitants as enemies and obstacles in the way of their advance, and those people still suffer the results. Vine Deloria, Jr., an American Indian activist, once wrote of the irony he hears in the song "My Country 'tis of Thee:" "Land where my fathers died, Land of the Pilgrims' pride" — yet most of his forefathers died trying to protect this land from the pilgrims and their kind.[10] Bartolomé de Las Casas would not want us to forget that the freedom and prosperity we celebrate in our country were often won at the cost of someone else's oppression and suffering.

He would also want us to remember what he argued against Sepulveda: that all people of the world are human beings, entitled to respect and loved by God. People whose culture or behavior or beliefs are different from our own don't deserve to be punished on that account; even our enemies aren't an evil for us to stamp out. And no one is naturally superior or inferior to anyone else. Racism, hate groups, skinheads and supremacist organizations seem to be enjoying a new popularity in recent years; but Las Casas laid all their arguments to rest 400 years ago in his debate with Sepulveda.

Las Casas also reminds us of all Christian missionaries. One Bishop in the Evangelical Lutheran Church in America recently spoke to a gathering of pastors about the way we have forgotten our missionaries. When he was growing up, he said, missionaries were a frequent topic of conversation at his church and in his family, and every child in the Sunday school could name a dozen or so. Now we rarely mention them. Today let's remember all the men and women who — like Las Casas — leave home, family and fortune to bring Christ to those who don't know him.

Bartolomé de Las Casas was a servant of Christ, the Prince of Peace. He understood that violence was never an acceptable means of advancing Christ's kingdom; that the fruits of faith are grace, mercy and peace, not exploitation, slavery and war. He also understood that Jesus Christ has filled his church with the power to win its victories peaceably even when armies fail. For his faith, his compassion and his example, we give thanks to God. Amen.

July 22
Saint Mary Magdalene

God Changes Us And Uses Us
Ruth 1:6-18
and John 20:1-2, 11-18

Today is the festival day of Saint Mary Magdalene, a festival that is new to many of us although it is part of the tradition of most Christians in the world. What's special about this woman, and why do we honor her with a festival of the church?

Mary Magdalene is mentioned several times in the gospels, usually along with Jesus' mother Mary. Her first contact with Jesus was when he cast seven demons out of her, and after that healing she became a devoted follower of the Master. She traveled with Jesus and contributed her own money toward supporting Jesus and his ministry. She went with Jesus on his final trip to Jerusalem, and was standing at the foot of his cross when he was killed. Mary was in the first group who went to Jesus' tomb; she was the first to discover the empty tomb; she was the first to see the risen Christ; and she was the first to report to the disciples that Jesus had risen from the dead.

Because she was the one to whom Jesus first appeared and the one Jesus sent to announce his resurrection, she has been called "the apostle to the apostles." Having been changed and redeemed by the power of God in Christ, Mary Magdalene went on to play a central role in carrying out Jesus' ministry and in spreading the Gospel. Small wonder, then, that we remember her with a special day on our calendar.

The First Lesson for St. Mary Magdalene's Day is the touching story of Ruth. Ruth was another young woman who suffered a bitter affliction. She was a childless widow, cast adrift in a foreign land with her mother-in-law, who was also a lonely widow. But the power of God changed Ruth's life, too, and she became part of God's plan to save his people. In the two stories of Ruth and Mary Magdalene, we can discern a pattern that shapes our own lives: God changes us and uses us.

First, God's love has the power to change people. Ruth and Naomi were both devastated by their misfortunes. Naomi had been driven from her home by famine, and lost her husband and both her sons while living far from home. Naomi was left husbandless and childless, and both her daughters-in-law were left young widows. Their grief was oppressive. In those days, women belonged to their husbands, their prestige was measured by their sons, and they had no means to support themselves. Widows were outcasts, and usually compelled to beg for a living. Naomi and Ruth faced a dreadful life when they returned to Bethlehem. Naomi even changed her name from Naomi, which means "good favor," to Mara, which means "bitterness."

But in the middle of that grief, bitterness and hopelessness, the beauty of love shone. Ruth and Naomi were bound by love, and Ruth refused a chance to go home to Moab and remarry, choosing instead to go to Bethlehem with Naomi. Back in Bethlehem, Ruth worked to collect food for them both, while Naomi kept an eye open to find Ruth a husband. Although Naomi alleged that the hand of the Lord had afflicted her, in the devotion of Ruth the hand of the Lord cared for Naomi and relieved both women's bitterness. Ruth eventually married Naomi's kinsman Boaz and became the grandmother of King David.

Mary Magdalene's story is similar. Luke reports that she was possessed by seven demons. It is unclear whether she was tormented by a whole band of devils at once, or by one devil after another; either way, her suffering was horrible. Demon possession for ancient people could mean physical disease, mental illness, wickedness and guilt, condemnation, ostracism — and Mary had a seven-fold dose of it. But Jesus had compassion on her and cast out her demons, restoring her to health, peace of mind and a respectable place among her people. Mary, free from her demons, then followed after Jesus, helped him in his ministry, supported his mission financially and became the principal witness to his empty tomb and resurrection. God's compassion changed her from a tortured demoniac to a child of the resurrection and a messenger of hope to the world.

The pattern of God's love in the lives of Ruth and Mary Magdalene holds true in our lives, too. Our relationships are given to us through God's love. When husbands and wives care for each other, when parents provide for their children, when friends look after each other's best interests, the love of God is working just as it did in Ruth's love for Naomi. That love can build friendship, cure loneliness, encourage people who are broken-hearted, find help for the needy; it can change bitterness into hope.

God's love also casts out our demons. Sin possesses us all and makes us guilty; guilt makes us feel helpless and unworthy. The guilt and desperation that result from our sinfulness can lead us to addiction, alcoholism, thoughts of suicide. Or rather than surrendering to our low self-esteem we may seek ways to raise it, and turn to material pleasures, sensualism, racism or hypocrisy. We have hardly begun to number our demons by the time we count seven.

But God has power over all those demons: the power of forgiveness. When you are forgiven, your past and your shortcomings don't exist anymore, so they can't haunt and possess you or drive you to despair. And once the guilt-demon is sent packing, you begin to be liberated from the rest of the demons as well.

In 1984 the town of Barneveld, Wisconsin, was destroyed by a tornado. The people of the town lost everything: their homes, their schools, their church; some loved ones; even some of their children. But they used the loss as an opportunity to create new relationships. The churches in town cooperated in a rebuilding program. The people of Barneveld strengthened and supported and assisted each other throughout the tragedy. God's love has that power, the power to give hope and a new life in desperate times. God can remake our lives just as the townspeople rebuilt Barneveld.

These stories also tell us that once God has changed us, he uses us as agents of his purpose. The love that changed Ruth's life led her to minister to Naomi. The love that healed Mary Magdalene drew her to Jesus as a disciple and apostle. And God uses us in the same way.

You probably know someone who is lonely, like Naomi. You probably know someone who is grieving, discouraged or unemployed. Perhaps you know of people in your community who are homeless. There's a saying, that when you need something you should ask God and ask God's people. And when you ask God, it's through his people that God answers. You and I are God's people, so when God sees someone in need he ministers to that need through you and me.

You also know people with spiritual needs — friends, neighbors, family members who need to learn about God's love for them and the risen Lord who saves them from death. The love that changed Mary Magdalene's life made her a co-worker with Jesus in his ministry and a witness to his resurrection, and God has called you to that same ministry through your baptism.

A man regularly rode a certain subway train in New York. Everyday he walked up and down the aisle of the car and told people, "If you have eye trouble see Doctor Clark in Manhattan. I was blind, and he restored my sight. He's the greatest." He wanted to tell the whole world about the gift he had received and pay tribute to the doctor who had worked such a miracle. Mary Magdalene received a gift like that, and you and I have received one also. Our gratitude and joy naturally make us want to share our good news with other people who could benefit from our experience.

However, many of us feel that we aren't capable of serving as God's ministers. We're not smart enough, or too shy, or too awkward, or too sinful to be part of God's mission. Well, look at Ruth: she was penniless, a pagan, a foreigner. And Mary was a lunatic, possessed by the devil. If God can use them, he can use any of us.

Once there was a sculptor who was getting old. He had arthritis, his sight was growing dim, and the quality of his sculpture was declining. His son, who was also an artist, invited the old man to share his studio, and it broke his heart to see his father struggling to overcome the loss of his talent. So every night after the father was in bed, his son took the figures he was working on and reworked them, sharpening their lines and adding fine details. The father never knew what was happening, but he was delighted that his talent seemed to have returned, and he lived out his days contented.

That's the way our gifts work. You don't need to save any souls, or give hope to anyone in despair: God does that. You and I lack the power to change lives. But God can take our clumsy efforts and carry them to success.

God uses his power to change our lives, to make us what he wants us to be. And then he uses us to minister to other people. That is what we celebrate today on the Festival of Saint Mary Magdalene, the "apostle to the apostles." We celebrate the wonderful things Jesus did in Mary's life and the wonderful service and witness Jesus' gifts inspired in her. And we pray that the wonderful things God is doing in our lives today will inspire the same in us. Amen.

July 28
Johann Sebastian Bach, 1750;
Heinrich Schütz, 1672;
George Frederick Handel, 1759; Musicians

The Language Of The Soul
Psalm 98

Today we're commemorating three great composers of sacred music in the Baroque Era: Johann Sebastian Bach, Heinrich Schütz and George Frederick Handel. We remember them together because they lived and wrote in the same historical period and in a similar music style. And we remember them today because July 28 is the anniversary of the death of Johann Sebastian Bach, and Bach is clearly the most important of these three composers, if not the most important composer of Christian music who ever lived.

Remembering these composers helps us celebrate our great heritage of sacred music and reflect on the importance of music in the life of the church, but it also leads us to think about the relation between our faith and music, in particular, and the arts in general.

Heinrich Schütz was born in 1585, exactly 100 years before Bach and Handel, and 102 years after Martin Luther. Schütz was among the earliest eminent Lutheran composers, and helped create the great Lutheran tradition of choral music. Music had been near the core of the Lutheran Reformation. Luther was a music lover and a musician himself, and he knew what Madison Avenue advertising agents would discover 400 years later: that music is a powerful way to communicate ideas to people.

In the Catholic Church of Luther's day, only the priest and the choir sang; the people in the congregation just listened. What's more, the music was all sung in Latin, which none of the people in the church understood. So the musical parts of the service were prime nap time for most people in the congregation.

In Luther's church, music became the treasure of the common people. First, he restored the practice of congregational singing, and wrote many hymns and chorales that are still favorites today: "A Mighty Fortress," "From Heaven Above to Earth I Come," "Out of the Depths I Cry to Thee." He also introduced the practice of singing in German, so the people in the congregation could understand and learn the words. Most of the common people of Luther's time couldn't read, but they could memorize the words of the hymns they sang on Sundays, and sing them during the week at home as they worked in their fields; and teach them to their children; and spread the word of God in their singing.

So the Lutheran church was a singing church. And by the end of its first century in existence, it was developing a tradition of church music — choir and organ music as well as congregational hymns. Heinrich Schütz, who came along at that time, was a great composer of church music for the German people in the German language. His music is famous for its technical genius, but also for its sincere devotional quality. Almost all his music consists of musical settings of biblical texts. In Schütz's hands, Scripture and singing were joined together for the benefit of the common folk.

George Frederick Handel was a different sort of composer altogether. Handel is of course best known to us for his great oratorio, *Messiah*. Most of us would consider Easter incomplete without Handel's "Hallelujah Chorus," and Christmas incomplete without "For Unto Us a Child is Born," both of which come from *Messiah*. But Handel didn't write church music at all: all his music, including *Messiah*, was written for the musical theater. Handel started out writing Italian operas, and when he moved to England and his operas started to go out of fashion he wrote oratorios, like *Messiah*, which were originally operas on religious themes. His religious operas were enormously popular, and Handel lived out his life as a wealthy man.

That puts Handel's religious music in a different light, doesn't it? Doesn't it spoil the Hallelujah Chorus to know that Handel wrote it to sell concert hall tickets? Not at all. Great music is great music, and the proclamation of Christ and his resurrection is powerful in Handel's oratorios regardless of the musical setting for which he wrote them. Most sacred music, devotional art and religious books have been created by people who were trying to earn a living at it, and that doesn't diminish the beauty of the work any.

But Handel's music raises a more important question about the relationship between faith and the arts. Opera was a pretty questionable art form in his day, and many Christians didn't approve of it. It was fancy and frilly, and dealt with some of the more risque aspects of love and romance, and with crimes of passion and the like. If there had been fundamentalists and phonographs in Handel's day, I'm sure fundamentalist preachers would have been smashing and burning opera records and playing them backwards to find Satanic messages in them. So a lot of tongues were clucked and fingers wagged when Handel wrote operatic music with biblical themes — operas about Jesus himself, even. Still, over the last 200 years, Handel's slightly disreputable religious music has enriched the lives and faith of millions of Christians.

Our faith and arts maintain that relationship to this day. "Christian rock" music is an example, as are Hollywood movies about religious subjects and Christian literature in comic book form. It's all commercial and it moves close to the boundaries of good taste. Some people categorically deny that Christian faith is compatible with rock-and-roll music, or the silver screen. Others claim that all secular art, music and literature are somehow "humanistic" and destroy religious values. Those people need to remember how their hearts raced and the hair on the backs of their necks stood up with excitement and joy the last time they heard the "Hallelujah Chorus," and remember that *Messiah* was the big commercial hit of 1741 in the English musical theater. Nobody has to like rock music or modern art or schlocky movies, but we need to judge them on the merits of the ideas they express, and not call a particular art form anti-Christian simply because of what it is.

Handel was considered the greatest organist and composer in the world in his day, except one. Handel's own best friend said that only one musician in the world was greater than Handel: J. S. Bach. Though Bach and Handel were the same age, and wrote in similar styles, there is a stark contrast between them. Where Handel dealt with religion for the sake of his music, Bach always wrote his music for the sake of his religion. He always thought of his music as a way that he could serve God: at the end of nearly every music manuscript he wrote either "in Jesus' name" or "to the glory of God."

There has never been another composer like Bach. Nor has there ever been another figure who represented Lutheranism the way Bach did, except Luther himself. *The Encyclopedia of the Lutheran Church* calls Bach and Luther "the two most illustrious personages in the history of Lutheranism," and claims that Bach's *Mass in B Minor* is "the greatest choral work the world knows."[11] Robert Schumann, a 19th century composer, said once that music owes as great a debt to Bach as religion owes to God.[12]

Bach's music has brought a powerful proclamation of faith to people all over the world. A friend of mine who is a Korean

Methodist pastor knew few Lutherans in Korea and wasn't acquainted with Lutheran doctrines, but the first time we met and he heard that I was a Lutheran, he told me "Lutheran is very good." "Why do you say that?" I asked him. And all he answered was, "Bach!"

Growing up in a family that was musical as well as Lutheran, I always thought of Bach's music and the whole experience of faith as somehow inseparable. And as I studied both music and religion in college my appreciation of Bach and my awareness of the greatness of our church and its heritage both continued to grow, and played a big part in my decision to go to seminary and become a pastor — and eventually a church historian. Even earlier, during that stage most of us go through as teenagers when life seems baffling and depressing, the one thing I found that could always lift my spirits was the music of Bach. Sitting in front of the stereo listening to one of Bach's passions or cantatas, I couldn't help but be filled with the knowledge of God's goodness and Christ's love.

More than anything, it's faith in the overwhelming goodness of God and the saving death of Christ that comes through Bach's music. Bach intimidates most organists and choirs because his music is so intricate and complex, but for all the complexity of his music, there is never any confusion about it, never a note that seems wasted or unnecessary, never a weak point. It's like a reflection of God's creation itself, in which the immensity and the detail seem overwhelming, but nothing is extra or out of place. And for all the emotional intensity of Bach's music, there is never anger or harshness in it. Bach wrote only in love and gratitude for his salvation.

Karl Barth, an early 20th century Swiss theologian and aficionado of Mozart, once remarked that the angels in heaven play Mozart for their own entertainment, but admitted that in the presence of God they must play Bach.[13] The teachings of Martin Luther and the music of J. S. Bach are the Lutheran church's two greatest gifts to the world. And our tradition of church music is only part of the gift of music that God has given to his children. It's that gift of music, the deepest language of the human soul, so powerfully expressed by Bach, Schütz and Handel, that we celebrate today. Amen.

Florence Nightingale, 1910;
Clara Maass, 1901; Renewers of Society

The Only Way To Make Life Real
John 15:12-17

Today's two saints of blessed memory are more modern and probably more familiar to you than some of the people we've commemorated previously. Florence Nightingale was the famous English woman who, in the 1850s, shocked her wealthy and proper family by announcing that she wanted to become a nurse, which in those days was a job for women who couldn't find work as maids or washerwomen. She further embarrassed her peers by volunteering to be the first woman nurse in the British Army during the Crimean War, and almost singlehandedly made military nursing humane and efficient. After the war she returned to England and used the lessons she had learned during the war to establish modern nursing as a health-care profession.

Clara Maass might be called Florence Nightingale's American counterpart. She was also an early practitioner of clean, compassionate, modern nursing and volunteered for army nursing during the Spanish-American War. Her career led her into the fight against tropical diseases that afflicted servicemen, and she died at the age of 25 in an effort to stop yellow fever.

The lives of these two pioneer nurses are a two-sided reminder of what the modern medical profession is all about. When Florence Nightingale decided to become a nurse, hospitals were trash cans, a place to put away the sick and dying so their suffering and stink wouldn't offend decent people. Hospitals were dirty and noisy, antibiotics and painkillers were unknown. Nurses were menial workers who neglected their patients, ignored the orders of doctors (who often didn't much care, anyway), and were likely as not to be drunk on the job. It's no wonder that her well-bred family was horrified, and tried everything they could to persuade Florence that nursing was beneath her.

Medicine has changed in 140 years. To be sure, we complain about the high cost of medical care, and about doctors who keep us waiting, and about cold X-ray tables and immodest hospital gowns. But our complaints are trivial. Diseases that were rampant killers a generation or two ago have been eliminated or reduced to office-visit complaints. We may gripe if we wish, but we can't take for granted the advances in medical care that have been made since Florence Nightingale pinned on her nursing cap.

On the other hand, the commemoration of these nurses reminds the medical establishment — and our whole society — that medicine is a serving profession. Modern medical schools can train technically brilliant doctors, who can cure diseases that hadn't been discovered yet in the 19th century, more easily than teach them to care about their patients as human beings. "Holistic medicine" is a term in vogue — referring to medicine that deals with the whole lives of whole people — but it's sad that such a concept is still a novel idea. Holistic medicine is what Florence Nightingale was practicing in 1854, as she walked through hospital wards at night carrying a lamp, kissing the foreheads of young soldiers hallucinating about homes and families they would never see again, holding the hands of her volunteer nurses overwhelmed by the pain and carnage of war. Medical care is not just a technology; it is not just a business or a service industry; it is a humane ministry to people in need.

But the lessons we learn from our two nurses today go far beyond the medical profession. These two women were models of Christian compassion in all walks of life. They both chose nursing careers as a way to put their concern for other people into action, and both women declared that their self-sacrificing love of other people grew out of their faith in Christ.

Florence Nightingale grew up in a wealthy home full of pampering servants, but even as a young girl she would leave her home to go sit with poorer families who were suffering illness or tragedy. Once when her mother scolded her for staying with a sick woman rather than coming home for dinner, she said, "I can't sit down to a grand dinner while this poor woman is suffering so much and no one else can help her." When she was eight years old, her grandmother described her as "both Martha and Mary, two excellent characters blended."[15] Later, at the age when other young women of her social class were looking for wealthy young gentlemen to marry, she declared that "the only way to make life real is to do something to relieve human misery."[16] Before she left home to become a nurse, she conducted a school for the poor children of her town.

The life of Clara Maass is an even more dramatic story of self-sacrifice for the good of others. As an army nurse during the Spanish-American War, she saw the suffering and death caused by malaria and other tropical fevers. When the war ended, she volunteered to help the doctors who were trying to wipe out yellow fever. The goal of the research was to determine how yellow fever was transmitted, to stop its spread. Mosquitoes were suspected of spreading the fever and Clara Maass volunteered to let herself be bitten by mosquitoes to test the hypothesis. After her first voluntary bite she contracted a mild case of yellow fever from which she recovered. But she volunteered for a second test-bite, and died 10 days later. She was the only woman and the only American who gave her life in this research effort, which did eventually control yellow fever.

Jesus said, "No one has greater love than this, to lay down one's life for one's friends (John 15:13)." Florence Nightingale and Clara Maass set an example of obedient discipleship that few of us can hope to follow. And the people they served by their sacrifice were the people society turned its back on: the poor, the sick, the dying, maimed soldiers far from home, fever-stricken villagers in the Caribbean. In Matthew 25, Jesus suggests that the measure of the Christian life, the scale on which our entire lives are balanced, is our service to the least of his brothers and sisters. Someone else has said that the Christian life is like ripening grain: the more mature it gets, the lower it hangs its head.

"The Son of God goes forth to war," the hymn insists: "who follows in his train? (*LBW* 183)." You don't have to be a charity nurse or an experimental volunteer to follow in the train of Jesus. But a Christian in any profession, situation or walk of life is led by the teaching that Florence Nightingale discovered: "the only way to make life real is to do something to relieve human misery." Opportunities to relieve human misery are endless. You can help in a ministry to the homeless. You can give to the church's hunger program. You can be a Red Cross volunteer, or a hospital candy striper, or a blood donor. You can visit nursing homes, or be a big brother or big sister, or volunteer in a hospice program.

The Son of God goes forth to war against all human misery of the body, mind and spirit. Florence Nightingale and Clara Maass followed in his train, and you and I can, too, inspired, fueled and propelled by his Spirit of love.

One last thing these two women remind us of today is our freedom to do the unexpected, even the unapproved. Florence Nightingale did the opposite of what every custom and social convention told her to do. Nice girls don't become nurses, she was told, and she did. Women don't go to war zones, she was told, and she did. A single woman in a menial occupation can't change society, she was told, and she became a great hero and a pioneer of a modern way of life. Self-preservation is the single greatest drive of every creature, Clara Maass knew, and she intentionally exposed herself to a deadly disease to help save other people's lives.

Christians are mold-breakers. We do what our Lord tells us to do, not what our society or our families or our etiquette books tell us. And our Lord was the great mold-breaker of all time. Martin Luther King, Jr., once wrote that "Human salvation lies in the hands of the creatively maladjusted," a description appropriate of Jesus as well as of Doctor King, Florence Nightingale and Clara Maass.[17]

The freedom to break the bonds of the merely conventional is a great gift of the Christian life. Our self-esteem comes from being held in the arms of God, not from the approval of our peers. Our goal is the Kingdom of God, not worldly success. Our justification in life is the blood of Christ on the cross and nothing else.

Who follows in the train of Jesus? The creatively maladjusted. People who think and do what others tell them can't be done. People who place the needs of other people ahead of their own. People who know how to make life real. Amen.

August 15
Mary, Mother of Our Lord

God Comes To Us
In The Lowly Things
Luke 1:46-55

It may seem odd to you that we're celebrating Mary, the Mother of Our Lord, today in the Lutheran church. The veneration of Mary is one of those things we've always associated with the Roman Catholic Church that sparks tension between Lutherans and Catholics. Whatever historic disagreements recent Lutheran-Catholic dialogues have bridged over, we still don't agree on Mary's role.

Nonetheless, Mary has always been honored by the Lutheran churches in Europe, and many Lutheran bodies in this country have traditionally included the festival of Mary on their church calendars. Martin Luther was especially fond of Mary, and singled out her story for special treatment among all the stories in the Bible. In the character of Mary, Luther saw the whole gospel acted out.

Luther didn't actually think Mary was all that remarkable. He didn't praise her for being a virgin; he didn't believe, as the medieval church did, that she was perfectly sinless, or that Jesus carried her up into heaven after she died. No, the reason Luther considered Mary so special was precisely because she was so unremarkable. She was the perfect example of how God's grace works. She was humble, lowly, poor, weak and unrighteous just like everybody else. But God chose her to receive his favor and to be a blessing to the world. God "regarded the low estate of his handmaiden."

That's how God always operates: whatever blessings God gives, he gives purely out of his own gracious love, and not because anyone deserves to be blessed. God comes to us and saves us simply because he wants to, out of sheer undeserved love — the same reason he picked a nobody to be the mother of his Son.

Luther paraphrased Mary's words in the Magnificat this way:

> God has regarded me, a poor, despised and lowly maiden, though he might have found a rich, renowned, noble and mighty queen, . . . in order that no one might glory in His presence, as though [they] were worthy of this, and that I must acknowledge it all to be pure grace and goodness and not at all my merit or worthiness."[18]

Mary is praising God because he has chosen to bless her despite her poverty, her young age, her working-class family. Or, maybe we should say God has chosen Mary *because* of her poverty, youth and low social background. Another of Martin Luther's great statements was that "God always comes to us in the lowly things." Forsaking kings and queens and priests, God comes to us through a poor teen-aged girl engaged to a carpenter, nine months pregnant and sleeping in a barn, forced by a foreign emperor to travel to the hole-in-the-wall town of Bethlehem. God comes in a shivering, crying baby.

All through the gospels, Jesus passes up the powerful and wealthy and respectable, and chooses the fishermen, the tax collectors. He heals beggars, defends prostitutes. When he comes to town, whose house does he visit? Zacchaeus' — the most hated man in town. Why? Because, he says, "the Son of Man came to seek and to save the lost (Luke 19:10)."

God comes to us in the lowly things. God doesn't raise us up to his level; he lowers himself to our level — to the lowest level of humanity, in fact. If you want to meet God, you must look in the prisons, the nursing homes, the hospitals, the homeless shelters; you look where the people with the greatest need and the lowest status are.

Of course the other side of the story, Mary says, is that God has kicked the rich and powerful in the pants. "He has scattered the proud in the imagination of their hearts;" they've gagged on their own high opinion of themselves.

These words take dead aim at you and me. Nothing but our own pride keeps you and me from accepting the gracious love God showed to Mary. We want to deserve favor: we think we do deserve honor and distinction. Everyone wants to be somebody, and we all have standards of achievement or accomplishment or status or good behavior on which we peg our sense of self-worth.

We carry pictures of our kids to show off. And we look out of the corner of our eyes at what kind of car the people next to us are driving, and we know that they're looking at ours. We spend fortunes in barber shops and beauty shops, or on deodorants and cosmetics and stylish clothes, to enhance our image. We buy millions of books every year on how to improve everything from our memory to our love lives. And then we assume airs of false modesty when people compliment us: "Oh, don't carry on about me like that. You're embarrassing me. It was just some little thing I threw together;" yet all the while the praise we swallow is further fattening our egos.

God comes to us in the lowly things. He doesn't come to people who deserve him, but to people who need him. God comes to people crushed by guilt; to people starving for affection, or for food; to people with eyes red from crying, to people who can't decide if they're more afraid of living or of dying. To people who have to sleep in barns. God scoffs at our success, he's embarrassed by our little achievements, the things that puff up our own opinions of ourselves. So where does that leave us? Are we cut off from God? Does God turn his back on us?

No, of course not. None of our imagined importance or deserving changes what we really are. You could win the medal of honor and an Academy Award, and be named *Time's* person of the year, and to *Good Housekeeping's* most admired Americans list; and you'd still be what you were to begin with: a dying sinner; a weak, flawed, imperfect, frightened, lonely creature.

Mary calls all our greatness and worthiness and accomplishment "the imagination of our hearts." It's imaginary. We're fooling ourselves — but not very well. We all have moments of real self-awareness, when our pomp and pride let us down and we come face to face with our failures. We remember all the hurts we've caused other people in our lives, and all the times we've harbored anger against people who hurt us.

We look inside ourselves and discover how worried we are about what other people think about us, how afraid we are to reveal our true selves to others, how unable we are to love other people and to let them love us. At times we act brave and strong when we really want to cry out to someone for help. We have moments — maybe when a friend or loved one dies before we are ready for them to die — when we realize that all too soon we are going to die. And we fear either that our death is going to cause someone terrible grief, or that it won't cause anyone any grief at all.

And for all our pride, all our success, all our striving after respectability, we're finally just as lowly and needy as the beggars and prostitutes and sinners that Jesus saved in his lifetime.

God comes to us in the lowly things; he regards our low estate. God knows the weak places in our lives, the chinks in our armor, the times and places we cry out for love and forgiveness. He dashes our pride like the puff of fantasy it really is; and reveals us as the humble, dying sinners we are; and then he says, "You are whom I have chosen to save. You are whom I bought with my own blood and pain. You don't deserve me; you haven't earned my favor; but because I love you, it is yours."

God comes to us in the lowly things. Like the poor teen-aged girl, Mary. Like Mary's baby squalling in the middle of the night. Like the young man suffering on the cross. Like a bite of bread, and a taste of wine. God comes to us in the lowly things because that's where he can find us, and that's where we can receive him with no thought of our deserving or worthiness.

With Mary, we magnify the Lord, we rejoice in God our Savior, because he has regarded our low estate. He has come to us — lowly things that we are — and blessed us and saved us. Amen.

Augustine, Bishop of Hippo, 430

The Man Who
Fell In Love With God
Romans 13:11-14

Augustine was the bishop of the North African town of Hippo in the late fourth and fifth centuries, and is perhaps the most important figure in the history of the Christian faith, next to Jesus and the apostle Paul. The most important teachings of the Catholic Church and of most Protestant doctrinal traditions are rooted in the writings of Augustine. Martin Luther was an Augustinian monk, and was heavily influenced by the namesake of his order. John Calvin and John Wesley both drew on Augustine's thought in their writings. Our doctrines of original sin, of salvation by God's grace and of the church and the sacraments are all derived from what Augustine wrote nearly 1600 years ago.

But doctrines and theology aren't our main concern today, nor are the controversies Augustine settled in the early church.

When I think about Augustine, I think first of a man who fell in love with God — deeply and passionately in love with God. And that's what makes Augustine a great saint for us.

The modern world is often described as a secular world. In other words, modern people don't see things primarily in relation to God. God and religion are an important part of our lives, but one we often keep separate from other parts. One of the things we believe we need to do in life is to have a relationship with God, but we also need to attend to our jobs, our finances, our automobiles, our sickness and health and politics and other things that we don't consider religious concerns.

We chop our lives in different parts and strive for goals that lie in all different directions. We try to have a religious life, a family life, a recreational life, a professional life and a civic life. As a result we are restless, confused and divided. When we say of someone who has a lot of problems that they need to "get it all together," we are exactly right. Our frustration and our longing for peace of mind are the results of our being divided and pulled apart by conflicting goals and loyalties.

Augustine was a pulled-apart person, too, until he discovered that all his dividedness was actually caused by his being separated from God. One of his two greatest books was called the *Confessions,* the story of his spiritual pilgrimage and his conversion to Christianity. And he begins the *Confessions* by writing to God, "You have created us for yourself, and our hearts are restless until they rest in you."[19] But that realization only came to Augustine after a lifetime of searching and struggling.

He was the son of an ambitious middle-class father who wanted him to be successful and famous, and a Christian mother who wanted him to be faithful and devout. From the beginning he was torn between a father who encouraged him to compete and strive for success and a mother who taught him to be humble and penitent. Naturally, as a teenager he was more impressed by his dad's view of the world, and studied rhetoric so he could become a famous Roman orator, which was to the Romans what a Joe Montana or a Bruce Springsteen is to us. Along the way, he discovered that a rising star of oratory turned the heads of the young ladies. So by the time he was 19, he had a reputation as a promising orator — maybe headed for Rome itself — as well as a live-in girlfriend and a baby boy.

It wasn't long, though, before a new opportunity presented itself to Augustine, in the marriageable daughter of a prominent Roman family. So the young orator put his concubine on a boat to the far side of the Mediterranean and kept his son. He later wrote that sending his lover away was like tearing a chunk of flesh out of his own body, and that he mourned for weeks. But apparently a chunk of his flesh was a small price to pay for fame.

He was never to marry that Roman girl, though. He was beginning to realize that his life had brought him only misery and a compelling restlessness. No achievement, no friendship, no love affair, no public praise, no wealth in all North Africa had really made him feel fulfilled. So instead of going to Rome, getting married and becoming a senator, he turned to the study of religion. He joined a peculiar cult called the Manichaeans and discovered that they didn't have any answers. He studied the best of Greek philosophy and found hints there of the truth he was seeking, but it still eluded him. And the splitting of his soul, the war within his members that Paul had written about (Romans 7:23), grew more and more intense.

We can recognize Augustine as a person like ourselves, can't we? Looking at him, we see the youngster crying out for public attention and approval, the young adult preoccupied with wealth and upward mobility, the man in a mid-life crisis when his worldly success has left him unsatisfied; we see the sexual revolution and cults; we see philosophy and intellectualizing about the world. We see all the things people in our own time do to try to find wholeness and meaning in life. And at the end of the whole process we see a man who is beginning to think that the only way to put an end to his frenzied grasping for wholeness is simply to do away with himself.

But through all these years of struggling and searching, Augustine's mother, Monica, had stayed by him. And he had never forgotten her wishes and prayers that he would turn his life over to God and join the church. Since he had tried everything else, he thought he might try God. He began attending church and reading the Bible. He somehow knew that if he was ever going to be healed, it would be through faith in God. But it just wouldn't come. He wrote this: "A new will, which had begun within me, to wish freely to worship you and find joy in you, O God, the sole sure delight, was not yet able to overcome that prior will, grown strong with age."[20]

At the deepest point of his spiritual crisis, he pleaded with God the way he would plead with a lover. He later remembered his pleading this way: "O Lord, . . . arouse us and call us back; enkindle us and draw us to you; grow fragrant and sweet to us. Let us love you, and let us run to you."[21] His yearning for God was nothing short of a passion. He had discovered that only God could satisfy the longing of his soul. His sin was having other loves besides God, and his salvation was seeing that his heart would never be at peace until it was completely within the will and mind and love of God.

Only one problem remained for Augustine, but it was a terrible one. The God whom he wanted so desperately to love was eternal and bigger than the universe. Teenagers infatuated with inaccessible Hollywood stars are frustrated in love, but this man was in love with God, the Lord of the Universe! How could he have a satisfying and comforting relationship with someone who was the invisible, eternal principle of truth?

Jesus, that's how. That's what Augustine finally found in the Scriptures. Yes, God is invisible and eternal and universal, but he became a human being precisely so that we could see and feel his love and love him in return. Even that, though, could be a problem, since Jesus had been gone from the earth close to 400 years by Augustine's time. Could God still be seen and known and loved on earth?

Yes — in the church, which is the body of Christ. And in the members of the church, who are joined to the life of

Christ through baptism. And in the Word of God preached in the church. And in the sacraments, in which God comes to be with us: especially the sacrament of the very body and blood of Christ. Once the significance of the incarnation of the Son of God became clear to Augustine, he never lacked objects for his love of God.

Finally, his divided soul was healed. Now he read in Scripture that he could sell all he had and give to the poor, that he could put off the flesh and its impure desires and put on the Lord Jesus Christ. All the things that had pulled him away from God had no pull any more. Instead he felt the steady pull, the irresistible allure, the firm embrace of God.

And once he had fallen in love with God, he was able to love the world again, but in a proper way. Something Augustine taught that still sounds astonishing today was that there is nothing that is evil. God created everything; therefore everything is good. It is only our sinfulness that makes good things evil. Sex is good, the world is good, human society is good, food and drink are good, material possessions are good, except when we forget to see those things as part of our relationship to God. Seeing God as only part of our lives and other parts of our lives as independent of God is what is evil, and what causes all our suffering.

Overpowered by the beauty and truth and grace of God, Augustine fell in love. God, he wrote, is "the true and highest sweetness."[22] More than anything else, then, the commemoration of Saint Augustine is an invitation to you and me to feel the allure, the pull of God's love; to see the beauty of God — in fact, to see that only God is beauty; and to fall in love. Fall in love with God, with Jesus the God-Man, with his church, his Word, his world, his people. "You have made us for yourself, O God, and our hearts are restless until they rest in you." Amen.

September 2
Nikolai Frederik Severin Grundtvig, Bishop,
  Renewer of the Church, 1872

The Happy Dane
Matthew 7:24-27

One hardly knows where to begin describing this Dane's significance to the church. Nikolai Frederik Severin Grundtvig seems larger than life — including his name. He must hold the record for the longest name of a modern European hymn writer, but around his own house it would have been considered a poor excuse for a long name. His oldest son was Johan Diderik Nicolai Blicher Grundtvig, and as an elderly widower Nikolai married Asta Tugendreigh Adelheid Krag-Juel-Vind-Friss Reedtz, who must have snickered at his mere 11 syllables.

But Nikolai F. S. Grundtvig's list of memorable accomplishments is longer by far than his name. He is remembered as a prolific writer of hymns, a Bishop in the Danish church and a renewer of the spiritual vitality of that church. But he is also considered the great national poet of Denmark, the rediscoverer of ancient Nordic mythology, the founder of Danish public high schools or folk schools, and an author of democratic government in modern Denmark. He might be called the Jonathan Edwards, Benjamin Franklin, Thomas Jefferson, Horace Mann and Washington Irving of Denmark all rolled into one.

From Grundtvig's many contributions to the life of the church, it is possible to select four that have special significance for us today.

First, his commitment to orthodox Christianity. Grundtvig was ordained a pastor in 1811, when Europe was dominated by Enlightenment rationalism. Anybody of any scientific sophistication was scoffing at childish superstitions like believing in God or the Bible. Just 20 years before, the French Revolution had repudiated religion altogether. And rationalism prevailed even within the church, where God came to be regarded as the highest concept within the reach of human intelligence rather than as a personal being who created, loved and saved us.

From the beginning, Grundtvig rejected that kind of rationalism. As a young scholar he delved into the legends of old Danish mythology and argued that the stories of trolls, giants and heroes much better captured the human imagination and spirit than did the intellectualism of the universities. Soon, though, his interest in stories of the spiritual and the supernatural led him back to the old, old story of God and God's people told in the Bible. And his trial sermon as a candidate for ordination was a blistering attack on the Danish church and its clergy titled, "Why Has the Lord's Word Disappeared from His House?"

Quickly, Grundtvig became a leading defender of the traditional faith. His dedication to the solid faith of the church can be heard in his hymns, such as the well-known "Built On a Rock the Church Shall Stand," and "God's Word Is Our Great Heritage."

One stanza of "Built On a Rock" begins, "We are God's house of living stones (*LBW* 365)," which suggests Grundtvig's second contribution to the church. Grundtvig wasn't the only one defending the traditional faith, but many of those who welcomed his efforts were stodgy doctrine-splitters who squeezed all the life out of their Christianity by their formality and rigidity. Grundtvig believed Christianity had to be a living, changing thing that was renewed in the experience of each believer.

Baptism and the Lord's Supper are life-giving events, not doctrines of the church, he argued. So he soon had the conservatives as angry with him as the liberals. He went so far as to claim that the Word of God is not the written word in the Bible but the spoken word that comes alive for the hearers when the Bible is preached. That view is pretty well within the Lutheran tradition, but it has never set well with those who hold timeless truths more important than the living experience of God's love. Consequently, Grundtvig was refused a pastorate for 20 years by the church, and then spent 30 more years as the chaplain of a home for aged women in a remote village.

A third thing Grundtvig contributed to the modern understanding of Christianity was a respect for diversity and freedom of choice. The Danish church was badly divided up among rationalists, orthodox, a soul-searching movement known as pietists and the followers of Grundtvig. In the Danish state church, the country was divided into parishes; there was one church for each parish; and people had to go to the church in their parish — like geographical school districts in this country. A pietist who lived in a parish where the church or the pastor was rationalistic was simply out of luck. As a result, more and more people in Denmark quit going to church altogether, and Christian life was in a steep decline.

Grundtvig announced a radical idea: let people go to whatever church they wanted to! If the church in the next parish was more to their liking, let them go to church over there! Then everybody could find a church that met their needs, people would stay active in the church and all the different parties could coexist peacefully.

That sounds almost comically obvious to us, but in a European nation with a state church, letting people choose which church to attend was a real innovation. In fact even in America in the early 1800s, voluntary church membership was seen as a necessary but unfortunate result of having no state church. Most people feared that religion would decline in America since people weren't told where to go to church. Grundtvig was among the first to argue that letting people choose their church was not only tolerable, but actually beneficial for their spiritual lives.

And he was right. Once people were free to make religious commitments of their own choosing and to go to whichever church suited their own particular outlook, the vitality of the Danish church increased. And during the 1820s and '30s, observers discovered that the same thing was happening in America: voluntary church membership was strengthening, not weakening the churches. And we benefit from that principle today. We're all better off for having churches of all denominations and all ranges of styles within denominations in our community, and for being free to join the church whose spiritual vision seems most compelling to us.

The fourth remarkable thing we find in Grundtvig's life is joy. Grundtvig lived in a country not known for its light-heartedness. Ever since Shakespeare wrote his play about Hamlet, the tragic, brooding, "Melancholy Dane" has been almost a stereotype. In the church, the rationalists found no joy in anything, while the strict conservatives were harsh and unfeeling. The pietists in the Danish church were anything but unfeeling, but their feelings tended toward the gloomy and guilty, and they avoided celebration or gladness in their worship.

What a breath of fresh air Grundtvig's hymns and poetry were! "The Bells of Christmas Chime Once More;" "Bright and Glorious is the Sky;" "O Day Full of Grace." Even the prospect of death brought him joy:

When we on that final journey go
That Christ is for us preparing,

82

We'll gather in song, our hearts aglow,
All joy of the heavens sharing,
And walk in the light of God's own place
With angels his name adoring. (LBW 161)

Among Danish Lutheran immigrants to America the majority were either pietists or Grundtvigians. The pietists came to be known as the "gloomy Danes" and eventually became part of the American Lutheran Church; the followers of Grundtvig were called the "happy Danes" and were incorporated into the Lutheran Church in America. The two Danish traditions were finally united in 1988 when the ALC and LCA joined together; we might hope that if there were any gloomy Danes left, the reunion cheered them up.

Given Grundtvig's personal history of conflict and controversy, of being rejected by his church and criticized by his friends, the joy that he poured out in his hymns and poems is a remarkable testimony to the depth of his trust in God's care and Christ's power to forgive.

By the end of Grundtvig's life he was a national hero. He was named a bishop in the church, though he still wasn't made the pastor of a parish; he was elected to the national assembly where he helped introduce democratic government; he organized public schools around the country. His reforms had revived the church and helped it survive the social and theological storms of its age.

What was the secret of his appeal and his great contribution to the church? His naturally cheerful outlook, probably, along with a certain balance in everything he did. The rationalists celebrated human freedom and ability, but with no appreciation for the religious dimension; the orthodox defended the biblical faith, but with no passion for religious experience; the pietists had deep religious feelings but no gladness. Grundtvig was able to pick out what was best in each of those positions and to balance them in his own mind in a way that no one else could fully understand. And because he benefited from a variety of points of view, he learned the value of diversity of opinion and toleration of differences. His deep faith in God allowed him to find joy in the richness of his religious experiences, and his poet's soul enabled him to give us hymns that express both his faith and his joy. Amen.

September 4
Albert Schweitzer, Missionary to Africa, 1965

Practicing The Christian Life
1 Peter 3:8-12

The commemorations in this series have covered the span of Christian history from the days when Christians still worshiped secretly in houses to the 20th century; from dusty North Africa to the palace of the Grand Duke of Russia; from the hospital bed to the concert hall. We've commemorated heroic sacrifices, dramatic conversions, brilliant ideas and great art. We've seen how some of the great saints of the church put their faith into practice in the way they lived their lives.

Our commemoration today ties all those elements together in the life of one man, and brings them into our own lifetimes. Many of us can remember Albert Schweitzer winning the Nobel Peace Prize in 1952, and his death in 1965. But most are not aware that before he ever became a medical doctor or a missionary he was a great theologian, a renowned musician, a parish pastor and an important philosopher. If we can figure out how all those different pieces of his life fit together, we can begin to see what made him both a committed humanitarian and a challenging example of someone who followed Christ in the world.

Schweitzer was born in 1875, the son of a Lutheran pastor. At age 24 he received his doctorate in philosophy; at age 25 he received his doctorate in theology and was ordained a pastor. He first became famous for his book on Johann Sebastian Bach, which was published in 1905; even after he became a missionary in Africa, he remained in demand in Europe as a leading scholar and performer of Bach's organ music.

In 1906, Schweitzer published his greatest book: *The Quest of the Historical Jesus.* During the 19th century, European theologians had been obsessed with trying to figure out who Jesus really was and what Jesus really thought. Schweitzer's blockbuster book claimed that they had all missed the point. The important thing wasn't so much Jesus' teaching as it was his whole life and especially his death. The key to understanding Jesus, for Schweitzer, was that Jesus firmly believed the world had to end and give way to the kingdom of God, that he had to bring that about and that he had to do it by dying. Moreover, Schweitzer said, anyone who wants to be a follower of Jesus must also reject the world and live as if to do away with evil and usher in the kingdom of God. Since we have been baptized into Jesus' death and resurrection, we must live our lives as though we have already died and gone to heaven; only God's will and Christ's sacrifice on the cross matter to a Christian.

Schweitzer's book stood the church on its ear. He was suddenly the most important theologian in Europe; his scholarly career seemed secure. But the young pastor continued to surprise the religious community. If being a Christian means that we reject all worldly values and live as if we're already in the kingdom of God, he announced, then no serious Christian can spend his life sitting in Germany, writing books, giving lectures and collecting honors. In fact, before his book was off the press he had already decided to become a missionary, to devote his life to alleviating human suffering in the most needy place he could find.

So Schweitzer resigned his university appointments and his pastorate, abandoned his promising career and started medical school. The doctor of philosophy and doctor of theology became a doctor of medicine, and at the age of 38 left with his wife for Africa, where they built their own hospital.

His friends and the other great scholars of Europe couldn't believe he would do something so stupid. They referred to him as "the late Doctor Schweitzer," who for all serious purposes was dead and buried in Africa. He had broken his promises and deserted the people who were counting on him. Of course, 20 years later they were singing his praises as the greatest practitioner of the Christian life, but in 1913 none of his peers could understand what motivated him to do something so spectacularly absurd.

That's a pattern we have seen repeatedly in the lives of the saints of the church. Basil and Gregory and Gregory, the Cappadocian Fathers, all abandoned promising academic careers and gave away their family fortunes to become monks and priests. Vladimir of Kiev abandoned a life of conquest and plunder and gave away his fortune. Florence Nightingale turned her back on high society to become a charity nurse. Augustine gave up fame and fortune as an orator, as well as the prospect of marriage, to become a monk, priest and bishop. Clara Maass intentionally exposed herself to a deadly disease to protect other people from it.

All these men and women discovered what Schweitzer discovered: the decision to follow Christ must be a decision to reject the world as it is and to make the world what God wants it to be. In Mark 8:34, Jesus tells his disciples that anyone who wants to follow him must also pick up the cross of suffering servanthood for the redemption of the world. If we confess that Jesus is the Christ and that we are his followers, we obligate ourselves to live cross-shaped lives. That's what we've seen in the lives of our many saints; that's what Albert Schweitzer reminded the world in his 1906 book; and that's what his colleagues couldn't comprehend.

Schweitzer captured the attention and the hearts of people all over the world, partly because of timing. In the 1920s, '30s and '40s the world desperately needed an Albert Schweitzer. Schweitzer had only been in Africa a year when World War I broke out. It's hard for us to imagine what terrible things that war did to the morale of the entire world. It was the first truly global war; it was the first modern war, fought with chemical weapons, machine guns, airplanes and tanks; it was the bloodiest war in history at the time. Most important, it came at a time when people had been wildly optimistic about the progress of the human race. All the modern achievements of science and the human mind had led people to think that the world had become enlightened, that we advanced beyond barbarity, that the future was brilliant.

Then the war came, and slaughtered an entire generation of the best and brightest youths of Europe. All the optimism and hope of the world turned out to be lies. Several great historians predicted that civilization would end by 1920. The seeds of despair that led to Hitler and to the worldwide spread of Communism were sown in the ashes of that war.

In the midst of its horror, the world rediscovered Albert Schweitzer. Schweitzer himself was imprisoned during the war, but upon his release he returned to Africa and reopened his hospital. While the world raged with fear and hate, he went back to healing the sick and teaching the love of Christ. And he wrote about his work, so the whole world could learn his vision of peacefulness and respect for all people. A civilization that considered itself Christian but was still capable of consuming its own children in war was shamed by the example of the devoted missionary, but also comforted by the thought that somebody still believed he could overcome hatred, pain and death. He prodded the conscience of the world and inspired generations of people to take up the tasks of world peace and service to developing nations.

In Schweitzer's own view, the solution to the problems of the world was what he called a "reverence for life." All life, he taught, is holy and precious: not just human life, and especially not just one race, nationality, or class of human life. The idea that some kinds of life are expendable or that different levels of living things are more sacred than others, Schweitzer believed, is the source of the problems of modern civilization. God created all things with the same special care and continues to care for all things equally.

The world would be transformed today if people believed as Schweitzer did. No one who believed that every living thing in the world is holy to God would pollute rivers or oceans, or build parking lots over wildlife habitat. No one who believed that life must be preserved would participate in war; no government that held life absolutely sacred would spend more on weapon development than it does on medical research. No one who understood the value of human life would use or sell drugs or drive drunk. Terrorism, assassination and apartheid would be unknown in a world that revered life. Keeping food away from starving people for political reasons would be unthinkable.

Most critical problems in the world today share a root cause: we consider life cheap. We consider living things expendable if they stand between us and our worldly goals — especially things that live far away from us, or far down on the evolutionary scale. We need the vision of Albert Schweitzer as much today as the generation after World War I did.

How can we change the way the whole world thinks? Perhaps we can't: but we can change the way we think, and we can set an example by our own attitudes and actions. After all, Albert Schweitzer didn't set out to change the world: he only wanted to do the right thing with his own life. But his example captured the imaginations and inspired the hearts of millions of people. He showed the world what it means to confess that Jesus is the Christ, and to make that confession the guiding principle in one's own life.

Albert Schweitzer may be the most remarkable person we've commemorated in this series, and his commemoration is a fitting summary of our whole series of remembrances: his life combined a tradition of service to the church; the heritage of Bach's music; the theological brilliance of the Cappadocians; Augustine's belief in the goodness of all created things; Florence Nightingale's and Clara Maass' concern for the sick and needy; and the dramatic change of life that we have seen again and again. All these things that were part of Schweitzer's greatness grew out of his faith in Christ — the same faith that beckons you and me. Amen.

October 4
Francis of Assisi, Renewer of the Church, 1226

Romance, Reform And Vision
Luke 18:18-30

Francesco Bernardone was born in 1182 in the little Italian town of Assisi, and died October 4, 1226. By the time of his death he was among the most famous and beloved figures in the Catholic Church. Within two years after his death he had been canonized — named a saint. And Saint Francis is still remembered and loved the world over. He is known as a romantic: as a poet, a dreamer, a singer, a lover of nature. He is known as a reformer: a renewer of the church, a Christ-like reminder of how Christians ought to live in the world. And he is known as a mystic with a clear spiritual vision and a surpassing love of Christ.

Francis was a complicated man. Though he is deeply loved and widely revered, he is also difficult for modern people to understand or feel comfortable with.

The most attractive part of Francis' life is the romance. Francis was emotional, excitable, given to strong passions. He grew up in the age of knights and crusades, and dreamed of being a cavalry soldier. As a young man Francis was always falling in love and imagined that when he became a knight he would have a true ladylove, for whose honor and affection he would ride into battle.

Francis was also a troubador, a poet and singer of love songs. The son of a well-to-do cloth merchant, he was fond of dandy clothes and fine food. One of his friends wrote in a biography that Francis' real name was Giovanni, but he got the nickname Francesco because his father wanted him to enjoy the popularity of French music, poetry and fashion. "Frenchy," his father called him.

As a young man Francis experienced a religious awakening, after which he remained a romantic, though his passions had a new object. He still remembered his dream of being a knight in the army of a noble lord, but he came to understand that his Lord was Christ, not the Count of Assisi. The battles he was to fight, he now believed, were battles against sin, hopelessness and the decay of Christ's church. He did finally ride on a crusade against the Arabs, but as a missionary rather than as a knight, and on arriving in Syria he went unarmed into the Sultan's camp to preach the love of Christ.

Francis also loved nature and called all created things his brothers and sisters. His famous "Canticle of Brother Sun" praises God for creating our Brother Sun and Sister Moon, Brother Wind and Sister Water, Brother Fire and Mother Earth, and even Brother Death. Once when some noisy birds were interfering with his preaching, he asked the birds to be quiet and listen, which they did. Francis picked up worms in the road and moved them to a safe place where they wouldn't get stepped on.

Late in his life, Francis suffered from an eye disease that in his day could only be treated by cauterizing his eyelid and temple. As the doctor heated an iron poker red-hot to jab into his face Francis said to the fire, "My Brother Fire, . . . be courteous to me now, for I have always loved you and shall continue to do so for the sake of Him who created you."[23]

The history of our faith knows few moments that display such courage, faith and poetry.

What can we learn from Francis the romantic? One of his friends wrote that his chief aim in life "was to possess, outside the times of prayer and the divine office, an uninterrupted joyfulness of spirit, both outwardly and inwardly."[24] His poetry, music and love of life express that joyfulness. We often think of religion and romance as opposites and make our Christianity dour, somber, strident or passionless. For Francis, the Christian faith was a faith for passionate lovers, a faith that binds us to all that is beautiful in life. We can all learn to delight in the beauty of what God has given us, and to sing about it.

But Francis was also a reformer. "Reformer" may be too mild a term; he was a rebel who rejected the values of the society he lived in and whose whole life was a call to repentance.

The world of knights and nobles in which Francis lived was a world of pomp and arrogance. At the same time, a commercial economy was emerging in medieval Europe. People like Francis' father were discovering the power of money and trade. Some built up huge fortunes; others were left to beg in the streets; and the whole culture was obsessed with wealth. A book written during Francis' lifetime about manners and customs in Assisi was subtitled *Pride and Desire*.

Francesco grew up as proud and acquisitive as any of his contemporaries. But as he was becoming aware of the new direction of his life, he also became convinced that the conventional life of his peers was spiritually empty, even destructive.

The first religious mission he felt called to carry out was to rebuild a ruined church near his home. He took some of his father's cloth and sold it to raise funds. When his father learned of the theft, he took Francis before the bishop, who told him he must return his father's money. Francis not only returned the money, but renounced all his father's wealth, relinquishing everything his father had given him. He stripped off his clothes and walked out of the bishop's chambers naked. From that moment he rejected all worldly possessions.

For the rest of his life, Francis wore only the clothes and ate only the food he could obtain by begging. He pointed out to the people of Italy that they could live without all the things they thought they needed. After his followers became a major movement in the church, he wouldn't allow his order to own its own building or monastery; instead, they lived and worked in old ruins, in donated space in churches, or in the streets of the cities.

Once, when he was invited to an elegant banquet as the honored guest, Francis spent the evening of the banquet on the street begging. Arriving late at the feast, he produced a bag of bread crusts that he distributed on the plates of all the wealthy guests. His example humbled the host and guests, who gobbled up the crumbs the saint had shared with them.

The ladylove he had dreamed of as a young man he now identified as the most glorious, beautiful and honorable lady of all: Lady Poverty. To be the poorest of the poor was the most honorable quest he knew.

The other great vice of his age was pride and Francis rejected it as well. He avoided drawing attention to himself, and always humbled himself. If he were riding a donkey and saw someone walking, he would get down and walk so he would be the lowliest person present. As he lay dying, he asked his friends to lift him out of his bed, strip him and lay him on the dirt floor.

But he didn't devote himself to poverty and humility just to soothe his own conscience or to shame the wealthy. He genuinely loved the poor and miserable people of his society. As a young man, he once saw a leper walking down the road toward him. Lepers, in those days, were the most feared and abhorred outcasts in the human race. Though his inclination was to ride past the man on the opposite side of the road, something compelled Francis — to his own astonishment — to get off his horse, kiss the man's hand and give him some money. He spent much of the rest of his life living with lepers and caring for them.

Francis was also a friend of the poor. Even though he had only rags and scraps to live on, if he saw someone in need he would always give them what he had. When one of his companions made an unflattering remark about a disabled beggar who came to them for help, Francis ordered him to humble himself on the ground in front of the beggar: "When you see a beggar," he explained, "you must always remember in whose Name he comes, and that Christ took upon Himself all our poverty and our infirmities."[25]

The similarities between Francis' age and our own are obvious. The love of wealth and ostentation threatens to consume our society. We measure our worth by how our possessions compare to our neighbors; we measure our security by whether we have got enough things. The gap between the rich and the poor grows ever wider in our country.

Francis of Assisi reminds us that none of that is a proper object of our love. Only God and our neighbors matter; letting our attachment to things of the world prevent us from enjoying the beauty of God and other people only makes us miserable.

But we still haven't talked about Francis' mystical devotion to Christ. And that's the most important thing of all. That's what explains everything else about Francis. Francis saw everything in relation to Jesus Christ. He didn't love nature or creatures for their own sake, the way the ancient pagans did, but because God had created them. He didn't love beggars or lepers just to be sensational, but because Jesus loved beggars and lepers. He didn't humble himself and live in poverty just to make a point, but because the Son of God had humbled himself and become lowly for our sake.

The one thing that people of Francis' age — and our own — had the hardest time seeing in its proper relation to God's grace was their material wealth. Money and possessions seemed to acquire a worth of their own, which Francis strongly rejected. To benefit from Francis' example we don't have to renounce money and property altogether, but to remember that nothing in this world is worth anything unless we see it as a gift from our loving God, to be used in his service.

At the end of his life Francis in a mystical trance saw a vision of Jesus, after which Francis found wounds in his hands, feet and side like the wounds Jesus suffered on the cross. His desire to be worthy of his Lord scarred him just as Christ was scarred for us. More than his scars, however, it's his vision that makes Francis remarkable: his vision of God, but also his ability to see the truth about things in the world. The beauty of his vision gave him joy in life; the truth of his vision made him an example and teacher for the ages. Amen.

November 1
All Saints' Day

Citizens Of God's Kingdom
Matthew 5:1-12

All Saints' Day seems a proper day to conclude this series of commemorations of saints of the church. Today is a day to remember the saints who have preceded us in the faith as well as a time to celebrate our own sainthood, the transformation the Holy Spirit began in us at our baptism and will complete in us on our last day.

All Saints' Day originated as a day late in the year to commemorate all the anonymous martyrs and heroes of the church who didn't have their own days on the calendar. In more recent times it has become an occasion to remember all people who have died in Christ, especially our own loved ones. But we also look forward today toward the fulfillment of the promises Jesus made to the church and toward our own resurrection to eternal life. In each of these different ways we are reminded of the way our baptism into Jesus Christ shapes our lives and our expectations: we are reminded, in other words, of our sainthood.

Today's gospel, the Beatitudes in Matthew 5, is also about sainthood. "Blessedness," Jesus calls it, and he means much more than mere happiness or good luck. The blessedness Jesus describes in his Sermon on the Mount is the blessedness experienced by people whose lives have been entirely redirected, who have found a new source of value and object of devotion.

That new source and object is the kingdom of God. In the previous chapter Matthew summarized Jesus' preaching this way: "Repent, for the kingdom of heaven is at hand (4:17)." And in a verse that leads directly to his account of Jesus' great sermon he tells us that Jesus "went about all Galilee, teaching in their synagogues and preaching the gospel of the kingdom (4:23)." Apparently, then, the sermon that follows in chapters 5 through 7 is an example of the "gospel of the kingdom," and the saints Jesus is talking about are "blessed" because they have begun to live under God's rule.

Past, present and future are all united in the kingdom of God. The kingdom was inaugurated by the coming of Jesus into the world, and has been perpetuated in the church. It is present now as believers encounter Jesus Christ in the church and respond to him in faith and obedience. Most important, it is eternal, and Jesus' promise that all who believe in him will share the joy of life in the kingdom is the source of all Christian hope.

All saints — the great heroes of the church, the ordinary men and women who fill its congregations, you and I — have staked their lives on that promise. Some have already experienced its fulfillment and we celebrate their triumph; our own triumph, though yet to come, is just as certain. Who is a saint? A saint is someone who knows he will inherit the kingdom, who knows she will see God and lives as though those future events had already happened.

Anyone who enters the kingdom of God receives a new identity as a citizen of that kingdom. Saint Augustine, in *The City of God,* wrote that there are two great "cities:" the city of God and the city of earth. Christians, he wrote, are citizens of the city of God and only sojourners in the worldly city. They derive their loyalties and values entirely from their heavenly citizenship, and they always hope for the end of their sojourn and their final entry into the New Jerusalem, the heavenly city. Thus, even though saints live and work in the world under the power of the Holy Spirit, they are not worldly. Their vision always extends to horizons far beyond the world.

Paradoxically, the citizenship of saints in a kingdom beyond the world is precisely what allows them to live and serve in the world following Jesus' example. Saints don't depend on the standards of the world for their sense of self-worth or for their judgments of the worth of things around them. They are free from legalism, free from the need to prove their worth by their accomplishments, free from attachment to wealth and power: free to be humble, to make sacrifices, to follow the narrow and difficult path, to bear the cross of Christ.

Citizens of the kingdom of God also have a better perspective on the world. They can see the world better from the vantage point of the heavenly city; they can see it as it really is. The pure in heart, Jesus promises, shall see God: in other words, they will know the truth about God, as well as about themselves and the world. And knowing the truth they mourn. They mourn for their sinfulness and morality, for the corruption of human nature, for the cruelty and violence that persist in our society, for humankind's alienation from God, for the hopelessness experienced by people whose vision is limited to the world. But they will be comforted, Jesus says: their sorrow will be relieved in the coming age when the rule of God is complete.

Pictures taken by astronauts during their space travels often show a reversed perspective on the earth and its environs. Half the world looks upside down. The earth appears in the sky above the surface of the moon, shining brightly in the lunar night. Things look the opposite of the way they look to an earth-bound observer.

The citizen of the kingdom of heaven sees things in a similar reversed perspective. Things assume a different significance when they're illuminated by the light of Christ. The scale against which we measure the importance of things is inverted. While the world rewards pride, strength, cunning and assertiveness, saints of God desire poverty of spirit, meekness, mercy and peace. While the world teaches us to seek comfort and avoid pain, Jesus declares us blessed when we are persecuted. While the world praises nothing so highly as a good reputation, Jesus promises to reward those who are slandered and insulted.

So, is the life of saints a grim battle against the temptations of worldliness? Not at all. It is a joyful celebration of freedom from worldliness. Jesus doesn't suggest that his followers grit their teeth and endure persecution; he tells them to "rejoice and be glad." We can loosen our grasp on the world and its treasures because we have been given something much more precious. And once we escape our dependence on the world, we are free to love and enjoy our life in the world the way God intends us to.

All the saints we have honored in this series have exhibited the gifts of vision and freedom God gives citizens of the kingdom. We have remembered truth-seekers, peacemakers, agents of mercy. We have followed pilgrims on their quest for blessedness. We have learned to recognize the shape of a life that conforms to the will of God rather than the standards of the world. We have witnessed the ability of people who are free from the world to change it. We have seen men and women driven by their hunger for righteousness, and we have seen that hunger satisfied.

We marvel at those saints. We're humbled by their example, and we doubt that we can follow in their steps. Today we are reminded, however, that you and I are also saints. We have received the same baptism, the same Spirit, the same promise, the same faith that worked such wonders in their lives. We are members of the same communion, citizens of the same kingdom, children of the same God. We are reminded, too, that sainthood is not an honor to be achieved, but a gift to be received; men and women are made saints not by their piety, courage, or wisdom, but by the love of God. And in the new world that is coming we will join with all the saints in enjoying the glory of the kingdom.

G. K. Chesterton, the English novelist and biographer, offered Francis of Assisi as a model of a life lived by the light of the dawning age. *Le Jongleur de Dieu*, he called the saint: God's juggler, acrobat, jester.[26] Like an acrobat who sees the world upside down at the peak of a somersault, Francis saw the world with its purposes and values inverted. Seeing the world upside down makes everything appear to be hanging: so Francis saw all things suspended, dependent on God's grace. This reversal blessed Francis and his friends with what Chesterton called "a freedom almost amounting to frivolity."[27]

"Freedom almost amounting to frivolity" is an apt summary of the life of a saint: a holy joy that arises not from ignorance of the world, sin and death, but from knowing the truth about them and from knowing that there is more beyond the world. The kingdom of heaven is at hand today and blessed are those who live in it. Amen.

Notes

[1] *Lutheran Book of Worship* (Minneapolis: Augsburg Publishing House and Philadelphia: Board of Publication, Lutheran Church in America, 1978), pp. 10-12.

[2] Philip H. Pfatteicher, *Manual on the Liturgy — Lutheran Book of Worship* (Minneapolis: Augsburg Publishing House, 1979); *Festivals and Commemorations* (Minneapolis: Augsburg Publishing House, 1980).

[3] Pfatteicher, *Festivals and Commemorations,* p. 251.

[4] Gustav Schnürer, *Church and Culture in the Middle Ages,* Book 1, Chapter 4, trans. G. Undreiner (Patterson, New Jersey: St. Anthony Guild Press, 1956), especially p. 180.

[5] Herbert J. Thurston and Donald Atwater, eds., *Butler's Lives of the Saints,* Volume 3, 2nd ed. (1956; reprint Westminster, Maryland: Christian Classics, 1981), p. 110.

[6] Ibid.

[7] Jay P. Dolan, *The American Catholic Experience* (Garden City, New York: Doubleday, 1985), p. 20.

[9] Lewis Hanke, *The Spanish Struggle for Justice in the Conquest of America* (Philadelphia: University of Pennsylvania Press, 1949), p. 125.

[9] Ibid., p. 126.

[10] Vine Deloria, Jr., *Custer Died for Your Sins: An Indian Manifesto* (New York: Avon Books, 1969), p. 10.

[11] Walter E. Buszin, "Johann Sebastian Bach," in *The Encyclopedia of the Lutheran Church,* vol. 1., ed. Julius Bodensieck (Minneapolis: Augsburg Publishing House, 1965), pp. 170, 171.

[12] Laurence N. Field, *Johann Sebastian Bach* (Minneapolis: Augsburg Publishing House, 1943), p. 4.

[13] Robert McAfee Brown, "Of Horsehair, Catgut, and Sublimity," in *The Christian Century* 96 (26 September 1979), p. 912.

[14] W. G. Wilson, *Soldiers' Heroine: Florence Nightingale* (New York: Friendship Press, 1942), p. 4.

[15] Ibid., p. 4

[16] Ibid., p. 5

[17] Martin Luther King, Jr., *Strength to Love* (New York: Harper and Row, Publishers, 1963), p. 14.

[18] Martin Luther, *The Magnificat,* in *Luther's Works,* Volume 21, ed. Jaroslav Pelikan (St. Louis: Concordia Publishing House, 1956), p. 314.

[19] Saint Augustine, *Confessions,* trans. John K. Ryan, Image Books Edition (Garden City, New York: Doubleday, 1960), p. 43.

[20] Ibid., p. 189.

[21] Ibid., p. 187.

[22] Ibid., p. 205.

[23] Otto Karrer and Nora Purtscher, *St. Francis of Assisi, the Legends and Lauds* (New York: Sheed and Ward, 1948), p. 128.

[24] Ibid., p. 84

[25] Ibid., p. 83.

[26] G. K. Chesterton, *The Collected Works of G. K. Chesterton,* Volume 2, *St. Francis of Assisi* (San Francisco: Ignatius Press, 1986), p. 67.

[27] Ibid., p. 69.

Credits

"Built on a Rock," text copyright ©1958 *Service Book and Hymnal.* Used by permission of Augsburg Fortress.

"O Day Full of Grace," text copyright ©1978 *Lutheran Book of Worship.* Used by permission of Augsburg Fortress.

Dates and identifications of lesser festivals and commemorations from *Lutheran Book of Worship,* copyright ©1978, by permission of Augsburg Fortress.

Luther's Works, Vol. 21, copyright ©1956 Concordia Publishing House. Reprinted by permission from CPH.

Portions of "Citizens of God's Kingdom" originally appeared in *LEXEGETE,* copyright ©1991 Tischrede Software, and are used by permission.